THE WORKING MAN AND WOMANS WAY TO WEALTH

BY: MAC TURNEY

COPYRIGHT 2007, 1985
ALL RIGHTS RESERVED
By MAC TURNEY
FIRST PRINTING 2007

ISBN
978-0-6151-5795-5

Mac Turney
P. O. Box 537
Stanfield, Arizona 85272-0537

TABLE OF CONTENTS

SECTION/CHAPTER	PAGE
* FOREWORD	5
* IS AMERICA BROKE? ARE YOU BROKE?	9
* WE ALL HAVE TO LEARN HOW!	11
* THERE IS NOT A LAZY WAY!	13
* WILL MY JOB MAKE ME WEALTHY?	14
* FLOPPY SOLED SHOES.	17
* EVEN IDEAS TAKE WORK.	19
* WHAT WILL HAPPEN IF?	20
* INFLATION/APPRECIATION	21
* THE PROSPEROUS PERIODS	24
* CAN WE AFFORD A HOME TODAY?	25
* IF THE WHOLE WORLD WAS COVERED WITH LAND WOULD IT ALL BE MORTGAGED?	27
* ARE YOU BROKE?	28
* THE AMERICAN DREAM	29
* RENTERS THROW AWAY THOUSANDS OF DOLLARS A YEAR	31
* OH YES, THANK YOU	32
* HOORAY FOR OLDER HOMES	33
* FOR SALE – "CHEAP"	36
* BAD CREDIT? YOU CAN STILL DO IT	38
* YOU CAN LIVE IN YOUR OWN HOME – "FREE"	39
* A HUGE BONUS!	42

* SOME POINTERS ON THE CONTRACT (I'M NOT A LAWYER)   44

* LOOK IT OVER   45

* RENTERS DON'T HAVE TO BE RENTERS   46

* DON'T BE A HOME BUYER/LOSER   47

* REMODEL IT – EXPAND IT – CHANGE IT – REDESIGN IT   48

* OLDER HOME SKETCHES AND REMODELING IDEAS   50

* ANOTHER OPTIONAL APPROACH   59

* WE MUST SETTLE FOR LESS   60

* BUT – I WANT A BIG ONE   61

* LAND DIRT CHEAP   64

* THE NECESSITIES AND A SHELTER   66

* PICK YOUR FUTURE HOME   67

* EXPAND, REMODEL AND DESIGN SKETCHES AND IDEAS   68

* YOU CAN PLAN YOUR OWN HOME   85

* THINGS TO KEEP IN MIND   86

* IT TAKES A LITTLE EFFORT   87

* YOU CAN BECOME WEALTHY, TOO   89

* NOW YOU KNOW HOW   90

* YOU CAN DO IT TOO! DO IT! BECOME WEALTHY!

FOREWORD

WHEN I FIRST WROTE THIS BOOK IT WAS 1985! OF COURSE, IT'S NOW 2007 WHICH IS 22 YEARS LATER AND I AM UPDATING AND RE-WRITING IT BUT IT IS INTERESTING TO NOTE HOW NOTHING HAS CHANGED – AMERICA IS STILL BROKE! HOWEVER, THERE IS ONE BIG DIFFERENCE TODAY! IN 1985 I WAS BROKE! I HAD JUST SURVIVED A BITTER DIVORCE THAT HAD LEFT ME WITHOUT ANY PROPERTY, ASSETS OR CASH. I HAD A GIRLFRIEND WITH A SON THAT I NEEDED TO SUPPORT SO WE LIVED ON WHATEVER WORK I COULD FIND – WHICH IS PRETTY SCARCE DURING THE WINTER IN FLAGSTAFF ARIZONA. I HAD BEGAN WORKING MORE OR LESS FULL TIME WHEN I WAS TWELVE YEARS OLD AND I HAVE EVEN BEEN IN SEVERAL DIFFERENT BUSINESSES BUT I DIDN'T HAVE MONEY TO START A NEW BUSINESS, SO, MORE IMPORTANTLY, AT LEAST UNDER THE CIRCUMSTANCE, I KNEW HOW TO MAKE MONEY THE OLD FASHIONED WAY – WORK! EXPEND SOME ENERGY TRYING TO MAKE MONEY! SINCE THERE WEREN'T ANY JOBS AT THAT TIME OF YEAR AROUND FLAGSTAFF, I DECIDED TO WRITE UP A PLAN TO FOLLOW THAT WOULD ALLOW ME TO VISUALLY SEE AND READ SOMETHING THAT I HOPED WOULD GET ME OUT OF THIS SITUATION. I HAD MADE A LOT OF MONEY AT TIMES AND OF COURSE HAD LOST MONEY OR SCUANDERED IT AWAY SO IF I COULD WRITE DOWN THE TIMES THAT WERE SUCCESSFUL AND THE MISTAKES I HAD MADE JUST MAYBE I COULD GET BACK ON MY WAY TO WEALTH AND AVOID MAKING THE SAME MISTAKES AGAIN. BY THE TIME I WAS HALF WAY THROUGH THE PLAN I REALIZED THAT THIS COULD BECOME A BOOK ABOUT HOW TO MAKE MONEY THE WAY I HAD DONE IT – THE HARD WAY – THE WORKING MAN AND WOMANS WAY TO WEALTH – BY WORKING. SO I BORROWED A TYPEWRITER, BOUGHT SOME TYPING PAPER AND WENT TO WORK WRITING THIS BOOK!

WITHIN A FEW OF DAYS, BELIEVE IT OR NOT, I HAD A ROUGHLY WRITTEN BOOK TYPED. BUT THE SKETCHES WOULD TAKE MORE TIME SO I WORKED ON THEM FOR A FEW MORE DAYS. WHILE I WAS WORKING ON THE SKETCHES I ASKED MY GIRLFRIENDS MOTHER, WHO WAS A WELL EDUCATED, ARTICULATE LADY TO READ THE BOOK AND LET ME KNOW WHAT SHE THOUGHT. THAT MORNING I WAS LOOKING THROUGH THE NEWSPAPER FOR JOBS AND FOUND A COUPLE SO I MADE A PHONE CALL, WENT FOR AN INTERVIEW AND WENT BACK TO WORK. MY GIRLFRIENDS MOTHER THOUGHT THE BOOK NEEDED PUBLISHED BUT I HAD A JOB NOW SO I REALLY DIDN'T TAKE THE TIME TO PURSUE PUBLISHING THIS BOOK. AS I SAID ABOVE, IT IS NOW 2007 AND I'M NOT BROKE ANY LONGER! I'M OLDER AND RETIRED – BUT NOT ALL THE WAY RETIRED – AND WORTH TWO MILLION OR MORE DEPENDING ON WHETHER I SELL SOME OF THE

PROPERTY THAT I BOUGHT SEVERAL YEARS AGO TODAY OR SELL A FEW YEARS FROM NOW. I OWN A BEAUTIFUL 2,600 SQUARE FOOT HOME THAT I BUILT, EVEN THOUGHT I DID USE SUBCONTRACTORS FOR THE JOBS THAT I DIDN'T WANT TO DO, I HAVE RENTALS AND I HAVE PROPERTY THAT I HAVE SOLD AND THE BUYERS MAKE THE PAYMENTS TO ME. I WAS ABLE TO GO FROM BROKE TO WEALTHY BY USING THE INFORMATION YOU ARE ABOUT TO READ IN THE FOLLOWING CHAPTERS.
YOU CAN DO IT TOO!
YOU DON'T HAVE TO BE BROKE!
YOU DON'T HAVE TO BE A RENTER!
YOU WON'T LOSE YOUR HOME IF YOU LOSE YOUR JOB!
YOU CAN GET WEALTHY!

WHEN I WAS 17 I WAS IN THE MILITARY AND AT THE AGE OF 18 I WAS MARRIED AND RENTED AN APARTMENT WHICH COST ALMOST HALF OF MY PAYCHECK EACH MONTH SO I BOUGHT MY FIRST HOME AT 19 YEARS OLD. IT BECAME OBVIOUS TO ME THAT ON A WORKING MANS WAGES I WAS ONLY GOING TO MAKE ENOUGH MONEY TO PAY ALL THE BILLS AND SURVIVE AND IF I WAS LUCKY, IN 50 YEARS I WILL HAVE ACCUMULATED A SMALL RETIREMENT FUND PROVIDED I DIDN'T GET HURT OR LOSE MY JOB AND EVERYTHING ELSE THAT I HAD WORKED FOR. I DECIDED THAT THE ONLY THING I HAD TO SELL WAS MY TIME AND THAT IF I SOLD ALL OF IT THAT I COULD I WOULD MAKE MORE MONEY THAN THOSE WHO ONLY SOLD 8 HOURS A DAY AND THAT I COULD WORK FOR SOMEONE REALLY CHEAP TO LEARN SKILLS THAT I DIDN'T HAVE WHICH I COULD USE TO MAKE MORE MONEY. I WOULD WORK FOR SOMEONE ON MY DAYS OFF EVEN WHILE I WAS IN THE MILITARY AND SINCE I STUDIED ELECTRONICS IN A MILITARY SCHOOL I OPENED A TV AND STEREO REPAIR SHOP IN A GARAGE THAT I HAD RENTED.

AT THIS TIME I WILL DEDICATE THIS BOOK WHICH WILL EXPLAIN HOW I GAINED THE INFORMATION I HAD BY THE TIME I WAS 18 YEARS OLD!

MY FATHER, DADDY WHEN I WAS VERY YOUNG, DAD WHEN I WAS A LITTLE OLDER, POPPA AFTER I HAD KIDS WHO CALLED HIM THAT WAS BORN IN 1893 IN OKLAHOMA. MY MOM, MOMMA WHEN YOUNG AND MOM OR MOTHER LATER WAS BORN IN 1907 IN KANSAS.

MY DAD WAS ON HIS OWN AT 10 YEARS OLD AND HE SURVIVED! MY MOM ALONG WITH HER FIVE SISTERS LIVED IN A TENT WITH THEIR FATHER, GRANDPA FORD, WHEN SHE MET AND MARRIED MY DAD.

THEY WERE IN AMERICA WHEN VOLUNTARY DRIVERS LICENSES FIRST CAME IN EXISTANCE AND LATER BECAME LAW. THEY WERE HERE WHEN SOCIAL SECURITY WAS FIRST THOUGHT UP BY POLITICIANS AS A VOLUNTARY RETIREMENT PLAN OFFERED TO EVERYONE BY THE

GOVERNMENT. THEY WERE HERE DURING WORLD WAR 1, THE ROARING TWENTIES, THE DEPRESSION, WORLD WAR 2, THE KOREAN WAR, THE COLD WAR, THE VIETNAM WAR AND THEY HAD SONS IN ALL OF THEM EXCEPT WORLD WAR 1. UNCLE JESS WAS IN WORLD WAR 1.

AT, WHAT SEEMS TO ME, FIVE OR SIX YEARS OLD MY DAD WOULD GIVE US JOBS TO DO AROUND THE FARM WHERE WE LIVED AT THE TIME OR WHEREVER WE LIVED, EVEN IF IT WAS IN TOWN. SOMETIMES HE WOULD ACTUALLY GIVE A QUARTER FOR WORKING HARD, SHOWING UP ON TIME, QUITING AT QUITING TIME AND FOR DOING A GOOD JOB. WE WERE TAUGHT WORK ETHICS, SELF MOTIVATION AND DETERMINATION TO SUCCEED BY WORKING AND TO WORK WHENEVER WE TOOK ON A JOB EVEN IF WE WEREN'T ACTUALLY GETTING PAID FOR IT.

THIS BOOK IS DEDICATED TO MY DAD, MY MOM, MY BROTHERS AND FRIENDS WHO HELPED ME WHEN I NEEDED A SECOND PAIR OF HANDS AND THEY WERE, WELL, JUST THAT, FRIENDS. IF YOU WANT A FRIEND YOU HAVE TO BE A FRIEND! EVEN WITH FAMILY!

THANKS FOR THE WORK ETHICS THAT MAMA, POPPA, AND MY BROTHER CHET TAUGHT ME. THANKS FOR THE HELP MY BROTHER TED GAVE ME WHEN I NEEDED THAT SECOND PAIR OF HANDS. I KNEW THAT IF I AGREED TO WORK FOR SOMEONE FOR $1.00 AN HOUR THAT I SHOULD WORK JUST AS HARD AS I WOULD IF I WAS BEING PAID $5.00 AN HOUR, AFTER ALL, I HAD AGREED TO WORK WHEN I TOOK THE JOB DIDN'T I? BECAUSE OF THAT ATTITUED I COULD ALWAYS FIND WORK. SO I SOLD ALL THE TIME THAT I COULD AND WORKED AS A PART TIME HELPER ON JOBS THAT I WANTED TO LEARN. I HELPED ON ALMOST ANY CONSTRUCTION JOB I COULD FIND – DIGGING DITCHES, PLUMBING, ELECTRICAL, CARPENTRY, PAINTING, CEMENT, ETC. - I KNEW I WAS GOING TO BUILD A HOME OF MY OWN SOME DAY! I WAS A WORKING MAN MAKING WORKING MANS WAGES. I WASN'T MAKING THOUSANDS OF DOLLARS PER HOUR LIKE THE HEADS OF GM OR GE OR AT&T. I KNEW THAT I WAS MAKING A LIVING BY SELLING 8 HOURS A DAY WHICH PAID MY BILLS BUT WHAT COULD I DO BY SELLING 16 HOURS A DAY? WOW! I WOULD HAVE A LOT OF EXTRA MONEY EACH MONTH! I DID THAT FOR A WHILE AND GAINED A LOT OF EXPERIENCE IN MANY DIFFERENT CONSTRUCTION TRADES. THEN I QUIT THE PART TIME JOBS AND BOUGHT SOME LAND WITH AN OLD LOG HOME ON IT (BUILD IN 1903 AS A CITY BUILDING FOR FAIRBANKS, ALASKA AND LATER, WHEN THEY BUILT A NEW REPLACEMENT BUILDING, IT WAS SOLD AND MOVED TO BADGER ROAD DURING THE 1950'S).

HEY, I'M ALREADY INTO THE BOOK AND THIS IS JUST THE FOREWORD. LET ME STOP HERE SO THAT YOU CAN READ THE BOOK AND PUT THIS INFORMATION TO WORK FOR YOURSELF SO YOU CAN BECOME WEALTHY!

PLEASE NOTE: IT WILL BE INTERESTING FOR YOU TO BE AWARE OF THE PRICES THAT WERE COMMON IN 1985 AND FOR US TO DO A COMPARISON TO THE PRICES IN 2007 SO, WHILE RE-WRITING THIS BOOK, I WILL BE USING SOME OF THE INFORMATION FROM THE 1985 ORIGINAL WHICH WE WILL DISCUSS MORE AT TIMES THROUGHOUT THE BOOK. I WILL DRAW ATTENTION TO THE 1985 INFORMATION BY PLACING A (1985) IN FRONT OF IT.

THANK YOU FAMILY AND FRIENDS WHO GAVE ME WORK ETHICS AND EXPERIENCE SO THAT I COULD EARN MY OWN WAY, EAT, PAY BILLS, SURVIVE AND PROSPER. AND, THANK YOU GOD FOR THE MANY BLESSINGS YOU HAVE GIVEN ME AND THE BLESSINGS YET TO COME! AND, THANK YOU FOR ALLOWING ME TO BORN IN AMERICA WHERE WITH EFFORT, A LITTLE BLOOD, SWEAT AND TEARS AND A PRAYER WE – THE WORKING MAN AND WOMAN – STILL HAVE A WAY TO WEALTH!

IS AMERICA BROKE?

ARE YOU BROKE?

(1985) THE ABOVE QUESTIONS ARE IN EVERYONE'S THOUGHTS NOW-A-DAYS. AMERICANS ARE GOING THROUGH A DIFFICULT PERIOD – FINANCIALLY. THE COUNTRY HAS A HIGH DEFICIT; WE ARE A DEBTOR NATION, OWING MORE MONEY TO FOREIGN COUNTRIES THAN THEY OWE US; WE HAD MORE BANK FAILURES IN 1985 THAN WE'VE HAD IN ANY SINGLE YEAR SINCE THE 30'S; THE COST OF A NEW HOME IN SOME STATES IS UP AROUND $140,000.00 OR MORE; INTEREST RATES ARE WELL ABOVE 10%, AND; BOTH THE HUSBAND AND WIFE MUST WORK, IN MOST FAMILIES, JUST FOR THEM TO PAY THEIR BILLS, RENT OR HOUSE PAYMENTS AND TO EAT – JUST TO SURVIVE!

THE ABOVE STATEMENT WRITTEN IN 1985 SOUNDS LIKE WE ARE TALKING ABOUT TODAY – 2007 – DOESN'T IT? THE ONLY DIFFERENCE IS THE PRICE OF A HOME IS A LOT HIGHER AND INTEREST RATES ARE LOWER IF YOU HAVE EXCELLENT CREDIT.

YET, EVEN WITH ALL THESE PROBLEMS, AMERICA THE FREE – THE LAND OF OPPORTUNITY, STILL BECKONS TO PEOPLE ALL OVER THE WORLD: PEOPLE WHO WANT FREEDOM; PEOPLE WHO WANT MORE OUT OF LIFE THAN WHAT THEY HAVE WHERE THEY LIVE; PEOPLE WHO WANT THE CHANCE TO BECOME FAMOUS AND/OR WEALTHY; - PEOPLE WHO STILL HAVE A DREAM!

THOSE PEOPLE AREN'T ANY DIFFERENT THAN YOU OR ME! WE WANT THE SAME CHANCE, THE SAME OPPORTUNITY. WE HAVE THE SAME DREAM; WE WANT TO BECOME WEALTHY, TOO!

THAT'S INTERESTING ISN'T IT? IF YOU ASK PEOPLE ALL OVER THE WORLD THEY WILL SAY "AMERICANS ARE ALL RICH". NOT TRUE! WE DO HAVE MORE THAN MOST AROUND THE WORLD AND WE LIVE OUR DAILY LIVES BETTER BUT IF WE LOST OUR JOB IT WOULDN'T TAKE LONG AND WE WOULD BE BROKE!

MILLIONS OF PEOPLE WANT TO COME TO AMERICA SO THEY CAN BECOME WEALTHY YET YOU'RE NOT WEALTHY AND YOU LIVE HERE! DO YOU REALLY WANT WEALTH? YES, YOU MUST WANT IT! IF YOU DO THEN YOU'RE HALF WAY THERE!

TO BE SUCCESSFUL YOU HAVE TO WANT TO BE SUCCESSFUL. TO BE HAPPY YOU HAVE TO WANT TO BE HAPPY. TO BE WEALTHY YOU HAVE TO WANT TO BE WEALTHY. IF YOU WANT THIS – AND I KNOW YOU DO – YOU

HAVE ALREADY TAKEN A BIG STEP IN THE RIGHT DIRECTION – IN THE DIRECTION TO ACHIEVE YOUR DREAM! BUT, LIKE ALL OF US, YOU NEED TO BE SHOWN HOW, HOW TO MAKE YOUR DREAM COME TRUE, HOW TO BECOME WEALTHY!

WE ALL HAVE TO LEARN HOW

WHEN WE WERE BORN WE DIDN'T KNOW HOW TO EAT WITH SIVLERWARE, DRINK, DRESS OURSELVES OR ANYTHING – OUR PARENTS TAUGHT US. WE DIDN'T KNOW HOW TO READ OR WRITE – WE HAD TO BE TAUGHT HOW. WE DIDN'T KNOW HOW TO DRIVE – SOMEONE TAUGHT US.

LATER WE HAD TO LEARN HOW TO DO OUR JOB. WE WENT TO SCHOOL OR SOMEONE TRAINED US HOW TO BE A SECRETARY, LAWYER, DOCTOR, MECHANIC OR WAITRESS.

IN FACT, IF WE THINK ABOUT IT A LITTLE SOMEONE HAD TO TEACH US HOW TO DO EVERYTHING OR WE WATCHED SOMEONE OR READ BOOKS AND TAUGHT OURSELVES. WE MUST LEARN HOW TO BECOME WEALTHY, TOO. WE AREN'T BORN WITH THAT SKILL EITHER.

MY DAD – POPPA – WAS A HARD WORKER AND WOULD WORK FOR FARMERS OR IN THE CONSTRUCTION TRADES DOING ANY JOB THAT WAS AVAILABLE FROM DIGING DITCHES OR CEMENT WORK TO FRAMING AND HE MAKE A LIVING AND WE SURVIVED. HE TAUGHT ME WORK ETHICS AND FROM THE TIME I CAN REMEMBER I WOULD CUT WOOD OR DO SOME TYPE OF CHORES TO EARN A QUARTER. HE WORKED HARD MOST OF HIS LIFE AND WHEN HE PASSED AWAY HE ONLY HAD $700.00 TO HIS NAME.

WHEN I WAS ABOUT 11 YEARS OLD MAMA AND POPPA DIVORCED AND MY SISTER AND I STAYED WITH MY MOTHER. ONE OLDER BROTHER WHO WAS STILL AT HOME MOVED WITH POPPA. MY MOM GOT A FEW DOLLARS A MONTH FROM POPPA BUT SHE WORKED AS A WAITRESS AND IN A BAKERY TO PAY THE BILLS.

BY THE TIME I WAS TWELVE I WAS WORKING SUMMERS AS A HELPER WITH MY BROTHER CHET DOING CONSTRUCTION – ANY JOB HE WANTED ME TO DO AND WHEN SCHOOL STARTED IN THE FALL I QUIT SCHOOL AND WORKED FULL TIME AT CONSTRUCTION. I HAD A CAR, A MOTOR CYCLE AND A GIRLFRIEND TO TAKE ON DATES. I WAS DOING GOOD SO I MOVED OUT ON MY OWN AT 13 AND SHARED A HOUSE WITH SOME FRIENDS WHICH WE ALL CHIPPED IN TO RENT. THEN CONSTRUCTION SLOWED DOWN AND THERE WASN'T MUCH WORK SO BY 17 YEARS OLD I JOINED THE NAVY.

BY THIS TIME MY MOM WAS DOING PRETTY GOOD FINANCIALLY. SHE BOUGHT A COUPLE OLD HOUSES AND FIXED THEM UP AND RENTED THEM OUT. I HELPED HER WORK ON SOME OF THEM – A LITTLE – UP UNTIL I JOINED THE NAVY BUT SHE KEPT DOING IT OVER AND OVER UNTIL SHE WAS FINANCIALLY – FOR THE TIMES – WELL OFF.

AFTER FOUR YEARS DURING THE VIETNAM ERA IN THE NAVY I RECEIVED MY HONORABLE DISCHARGE SOME METALS AND A RECOMMENDATION FOR RE-ENLISTMENT FOR OFFICERS CANDIDATE SCHOOL. I WANTED MORE THAN $225.00 A MONTH WHICH AT THE TIME (I WAS 21) SUPPORTED MY WIFE, TWO KIDS AND I. DURING THE LAST YEAR I HAD BEEN WORKING PART TIME WITH MY BROTHER CHET IN THE APPLICANCE, REFRIGERATION AND HEATING BUSINESS WHICH WENT ALONG WITH MY MILITARY TRAINING IN ELECTRONICS, SO I WENT TO WORK FULL TIME WITH HIM FOR $100.00 A WEEK WHICH WAS A NICE PAY INCREASE. I HAD BOUGHT A HOUSE WHEN I WAS 19 IN VALLEJO SO THAT WE WOULDN'T BE THROWING AWAY MY HARD EARNED MONEY ON RENT. I SOLD IT TO MY MOTHER SO THAT I COULD MOVE CLOSE TO WORK WHICH WAS IN OAKLAND AND MY BROTHER TED AND I BOUGHT A HUGE HOUSE AND WENT TO WORK REMODELING IT INTO A DUPLEX FOR OUR FAMILIES.

I HAD PICKED UP A LOT OF TRAINING AND WORK EXPERIENCE AND I HAD LEARNED THAT YOU CAN'T MAKE MONEY SITTING IN A CHAIR DREAMING ABOUT IT. YOU HAVE TO MAKE AN EFFORT TO GET IT! SO I WENT TO WORK LONG HOURS KEEPING THE THOUGHT IN MIND THAT I DIDN'T WANT TO JUST SURVIVE FROM PAY CHECK TO PAY CHECK.

MY BROTHER TED AND I MOVED OUR FAMILIES TO ALASKA RIGHT AFTER THE FLOOD IN FAIRBANKS. I TURNED 24 THE DAY WE CROSSED THE BORDER FROM CANADA TO ALASKA – WE HAD DROVE THE ALCAN HIGHWAY IN A CHEVY VAN WITH OUR TOOLS. WITHIN AN HOUR ON THE FIRST DAY WE ARRIVED IN FAIRBANKS WE FOUND A JOB WORKING FOR AN APPLIANCE COMPANY. WE WERE HIRED BY THE FIRST STORE THAT WE WENT TO. AFTER ALL, FAIRBANKS HAD JUST HAD A FLOOD AND LITTERLY EVERY APPLIANCE WAS RUINED OR IN NEED OF MAJOR REPAIR.

I MADE A LOT OF MONEY SELLING MY TIME WORKING AND BY FIXING UP HOUSES AND SELLING THEM. WITHIN A SHORT TIME I WAS A PARTNER IN OR OWNED, FIVE BUSINESSES, OWNED MY HOME, SOME LAND AND A TRI-PLEX. I WAS DOING GREAT! I'M NOT SAYING THAT I DID IT ALL PERFECTLY BECAUSE I DIDN'T! WHEN I MADE A LOT OF MONEY I SQUANDERED IT, AFTER ALL I WAS YOUNG, AND I LOST A LOT OF IT IN A BUSINESS VENTURE THAT I DIDN'T KNOW ANYTHING ABOUT. THEN MY WIFE AND I GOT A DIVORCE AND I LOST THE REST OF IT. I STARTED THIS BOOK BACK IN 1985 AND AT THE TIME I WAS BROKE AND DIDN'T HAVE A JOB OR A BUSINESS. I MADE A LOT OF MONEY AGAIN AFTER I FIRST WROTE THIS BOOK IN 1985 AND MARRIED MY SECOND WIFE IN 1988 WHO CONTRIBUTED GREATLY TO MY ENDING UP ALMOST BROKE AGAIN BEFORE I DIVORCED HER IN 1995. TODAY I HAVE AROUND 2 MILLION IN ASSETS ALL BECAUSE I WAS DETERMINED NOT TO BE BROKE. YOU CAN DO IT TOO!

THERE ISN'T A LAZY WAY

I KNOW THAT YOU'VE SEEN COMMERCIALS AND ARTICLES AND ADS TOUTING BOOKS THAT SAY YOU CAN THINK YOURSELF RICH OR GET RICH THE LAZY WAY AND SO HAVE I BUT YOU AND I AREN'T DUMB, WE KNOW THAT WE CAN'T SIT IN OUR RECLINERS ALL DAY AND EXPECT RICHES TO COME FLOWING IN; WE KNOW THAT WE CAN'T JUST SIT AND THINK OURSELVES RICH EITHER. WE KNOW THAT WE HAVE TO TAKE SOME KIND OF ACTION TO ACTUALLY GET RICH, DON'T WE?

MOST OF THE PEOPLE I HAVE MET IN MY LIFE AND PROBABLY MOST OF THE PEOPLE THAT YOU KNOW ARE BROKE AND DOING A GOOD JOB OF CONCEILING IT BY ACTING WEALTHY. THEY DRIVE NEW CARS AND LIVE IN A BIG NEW HOME AND APPEAR TO HAVE SPENDING MONEY. THEY GO TO WORK EVERY DAY FIVE OR SIX DAYS A WEEK OR MORE AND THEY'RE NOT LAZY. BUT THEY LIVE RIGHT AT THE EXTREME EDGE OF THEIR BUDGET AND WOULD BE BROKE VERY QUICKLY IF SOMETHING WENT WRONG AND I'VE SEEN THAT HAPPEN MANY TIMES LATELY.

I HAVE MET A LOT OF PEOPLE DURING MY LIFE THAT WERE REALLY HARD WORKERS AND APPEARED TO BE JUST GETTING BY ON WHAT THEY MADE EVERY WEEK BUT THEY WERE WEALTHY AND DID A GOOD JOB OF CONCEILING IT FROM THE WORLD, FROM ME AND FROM EVERYONE ELSE AND THEY'RE NOT LAZY.

HOWEVER, I HAVE NEVER MET ANYONE WHO IS LAZY THAT WAS WEALTHY OR THAT EVEN APPEAR WEALTHY. THEY DON'T HAVE ANYTHING THAT ISN'T GIVEN TO THEM; THEY LIVE WITH SOMEONE OR OFF OF SOMEONE ELSES MONEY AND THAT PERSON MAY WORK REALLY HARD FOR THEIR MONEY. LAZYNESS IS AS HARD A HABIT TO BREAK AS A DRUG ADDICTION AND THE ONLY WAY TO BREAK IT IS TO STOP!

EVEN THE ONES I HAVE MET THAT REALLY ARE WEALTHY HAVE WORK ETHICS AND THEY PUT OUT EFFORT EVERY DAY TO KEEP UP THEIR PROPERTY, MAKE MORE MONEY OR TO STAY WEALTHY BY NOT LOSING WHAT THEY ALREADY HAVE.

ONE DIFFERENCE BETWEEN THE WEALTHY AND THE POOR IS THE WEALTHY HAVE MORE TO LOSE IF SOMETHING GOES WRONG. SO, ONCE YOU READ THIS BOOK AND YOU'VE WORKED HARD TO ACCUMULATE SOME WEALTH, DON'T GET LAZY AND LOSE IT.

YOU'LL NEVER GET WEALTHY BY BEING LAZY BUT YOU KNOW THAT OR YOU WOULDN'T HAVE BOUGHT THIS BOOK.

WILL MY JOB MAKE ME WEALTHY?

YOU ALREADY KNOW THAT YOU CAN'T GO TO WORK DIGGING DITCHES ALL DAY AND GET WEALTHY; WE CAN'T SERVE FOOD TO CUSTOMERS EVERY DAY; WE CAN'T FIX SOMEONES CAR EVERY DAY; WE CAN'T TOW CARS EVERY DAY, OR; PUSH THE BUTTONS ON A KEYBOARD OR CASH REGISTER EITHER. YOU'VE ALREADY BEEN DOING THAT AND YOU ARE JUST SURVIVING AREN'T YOU? OUR JOB WILL NOT GET US WEALTHY, IN MOST CASES, BUT WE NEED TO KEEP THAT JOB BECAUSE IT PAYS THE BILLS.

HAVE YOU EVER FIGURED OUT WHAT YOU WILL MAKE IN YOUR LIFETIME DOING THE JOB YOU ARE DOING RIGHT NOW? GO AHEAD, ADD IT UP.

IF YOU ARE MAKEING $8.00 AN HOUR YOU WILL MAKE APPROXIMATELY $16,640.00 PER YEAR; $166,400.00 IN 10 YEARS; $832,000.00 IN 50 YEARS. IF YOU MAKE $12.00 PER HOUR YOU WILL MAKE APPROXIMATELY $24,960.00 PER YEAR; $249,600.00 IN 10 YEARS; $1,248,000.00 IN 50 YEARS. SURE, THE 50 YEAR FIGURE LOOKS AWFULLY GOOD AND IT WOULD BE IF YOU HAD ALL THE MONEY AT ONE TIME BUT YOU DON'T. THAT AMOUNT IS SPREAD OUT OVER A 50 YEAR PERIOD. DURING THAT TIME YOU ARE PAYING TAXES, RENT, UTILITIES, BUYING CARS, BUYING GAS, PAYING FOR INSURANCE, AUTO REPAIRS, FOOD, FURNITURE, CLOTHES, SENDING THE KIDS TO SCHOOL AND PAYING FOR ALL THE OTHER NECESSITIES OF LIFE. HAVE YOU EVER ASKED, "WHERE DID MY PAYCHECK GO?"

(1985) DID YOU KNOW THAT ACCORDING TO GOVERNMENT ESTIMATES IT COST YOU OVER $240,000.00 TO RAISE A BOY AND SEND HIM TO COLLEGE? WHAT HAPPENS TO THAT 50 YEARS OF INCOME IF YOU HAVE 4 BOYS? WAIT A MINUTE LADIES – IT COST MORE TO RAISE A GIRL! IF YOU HAVE FOUR CHILDREN – 2 BOYS AND 2 GIRLS, IT COST YOU A MILLION DOLLARS TO RAISE YOUR KIDS AND SEND THEM TO COLLEGE. WOW! SO IF YOU'RE MAKING THE $12. PER HOUR BY THE TIME YOU RAISE THE KIDS YOU ONLY HAVE $248,000.00 LEFT AFTER ALL THAT TIME. WAIT A MINUTE – YOU HAVE TO PAY RENT TOO! DO YOU HAVE ENOUGH FOR RENT? NO!

(1985). WHEN YOU RENT EVEN IF YOU ONLY PAY $400.00 PER MONTH YOU WILL THROW AWAY $4,800.00 PER YEAR; $48,000.00 IN TEN YEARS, AND; ABOUT $288,000.00 IN YOUR LIFETIME (SAY, AGE 20 TO 80). THERE ISN'T ANYTHING LEFT OVER FOR THE OTHER NECESSITIES IS THERE? WE MUST MAKE MORE MONEY THAN THAT SO WE WORK MORE HOURS, BOTH HUSBAND AND WIFE GO TO WORK, THE KIDS TAKE ON NEWSPAPER ROUTES – WORK – WORK – WORK!

THE SECRET IS: DON'T START LIVING BETTER – BEYOND YOUR MEANS – IF YOU DO YOU WILL ALWAYS BE BROKE!

THE AVERAGE MAN AND WOMAN ARE TOO BUSY WORKING – TRYING TO MAKE A LIVING – TO EVER GET RICH! BUT DARN IT WE HAVE TO WORK TO EAT AND PAY THE BILLS. WE CAN'T AFFORD TO TRY TO THINK OURSELVES RICH OR BE LAZY AND GET RICH. WE'RE DOING THE RIGHT THING! WE'RE CARRYING OUR OWN LOAD! WE'RE SENDING THE KIDS TO SCHOOL SO THEY CAN DO BETTER THAN WE DID! WE ARE LIVING COMFORTABLY EVEN THOUGH IT IS ON A TIGHT BUDGET.

THERE ARE ONLY SO MANY HOURS IN A DAY SO WE CAN'T EXPECT TO GET RICH BY TAKING ON ANOTHER JOB! WELL, CAN WE? MAYBE YOU CAN AND THE SECRET MIGHT BE: DON'T UPGRADE YOUR LIFESTYLE WITH THE EXTRA MONEY! DON'T RENT A BIGGER, MORE EXPENSIVE, HOUSE! DON'T BUY MORE TOYS! DON'T GO IN DEBT TO KEEP UP WITH THE JONESES!

YOU NEED TO SAVE THE EXTRA MONEY SO YOU WILL BE ABLE TO TAKE ADVANTAGE OF THE OPPORTUNITIES AVAILABLE AS WE ARE DISCUSSING IN THIS BOOK.

MANY DIVORCES AND UNHAPPY MARRIAGES ARE THE DIRECT RESULT OF NOT ENOUGH MONEY AND/OR NEVER SEEING EACH OTHER BECAUSE OF WORK. YOU BOTH NEED TO AGREE ON A PLAN OF ACTION TO BECOME WEALTHY AND STICK TO IT. MAYBE YOU ONLY NEED A FEW YEARS OF STICKING TO THE PLAN BUT IT CAN BE DONE AND YOU CAN BECOME WEALTHY TOO.

THINK ABOUT IT.

THE ONLY THING I HAVE TO SELL IS TIME AND IF I ONLY MAKE $10.00 AN HOUR FOR 40 HOURS A WEEK I WILL EARN $400.00 PER WEEK. IF IT TAKES $390.00 A WEEK FOR ME TO LIVE, PAY TAXES AND PAY THE BILLS I PROBABLY WILL NEVER GET RICH FROM MY JOB. BUT I HAVE TO SURVIVE SO I HAVE TO WORK, RIGHT? ABSOLUTELY! YOU MUST ALSO LIVE WITHIN YOUR BUDGET OF $400.00 A WEEK AND MANY AMERICANS DO THAT. BUT A LOT OF THEM GO IN DEBT AND PAY PAYMENTS FROM THEIR PAY CHECK ON EXTRA "TOYS" THEY WANT. NOW THEY ARE STRADDLED WITH PAYMENTS WHICH MUST BE MADE LONG AFTER THE "TOYS" HAVE WORN OUT. THEY MAKE THE RICH, WHO LOANED THEM THE MONEY, RICHER AND THEY STAY BROKE.

SOMEONE ASKED, "WHAT IS THE GAME OF LIFE?" I GUESS THE ANSWER IS, "HE WHO DIES WITH THE MOST TOYS WINS!"

ACTUALLY ONE OF THE MAIN TIPS ABOUT HOW TO GET WEALTHY IS ABOUT TO BE REVEALED: DON'T TRY TO KEEP UP WITH THE JONESES! LIVE WITHIN YOUR BUDGET – THE PAY FROM YOUR JOB!

WITH THAT IN MIND – YOU CAN START TO BECOME WEALTHY.

IF THE ONLY THING YOU HAVE TO SELL IS TIME AND YOU ARE SELLING 40 HOURS A WEEK AND YOU ARE LIVING ON THAT INCOME THEN SELL SOME MORE TIME! GET A PART TIME JOB! YOU ARE YOUNG SO YOU BETTER DO IT NOW BEFORE YOU'RE TOO OLD TO WORK THAT MANY HOURS. NOW YOU HAVE SPARE MONEY BUT DON'T GO OUT AND BUY MORE TOYS. KEEP IT AND LOOK FOR THE OPPORTUNITIES YOU ARE READING ABOUT IN THIS BOOK. ONCE YOU FIND IT YOU WILL HAVE THE MONEY TO BUY IT AND BECOME WEALTHY.

JUST ASK YOURSELF ONE QUESTION: IF I LOST MY JOB WOULD I LOSE MY CAR IN A FEW MONTHS, WOULD I LOSE MY HOME AFTER A PROLONGED TIME WITHOUT A JOB?

IF YOU ANSWERED YES – YOU ARE BROKE!

FLOPPY SOLED SHOES

NOT TOO MANY YEARS AGO MOST AMERICANS WERE POOR. WE DROVE OLD CARS OR STILL USED A HORSE AND WAGON. I REMEMBER GOING TO VISIT MY UNCLE, AUNT AND COUSINS WHEN I WAS A KID WHICH TOOK US ALL DAY TO GO 30 MILES WITH OUR HORSE AND WAGON IN THE MID FOURTIES. EVERYONE WE KNEW WAS POOR LIKE US. THERE WERE THE WEALTHY PEOPLE – I GUESS – AND THERE WERE THE POOR. THERE WERE PEOPLE WHO ATE WHAT THEY GREW AT HOME, WORE WORN OUT CLOTHES OR CLOTHES MADE FROM FLOUR SACKS AND WORE FLOPPY SOLED SHOES TO SCHOOL. WE WERE LIKE THAT! MY POPPA DID FARM WORK OR WORKED AT WHATEVER CAME ALONG WHEN HE COULD. US KIDS, WHO STILL LIVED AT HOME, HAD TO GO BAREFOOT DURING THE SUMMER AND SAVED OUT LAST YEARS SHOES FOR SCHOOL IN THE FALL. MINE WERE FLOPPY SOLED MOST YEARS. WE GOT NEW SHOES FOR CHRISTMAS MOST OF THE TIME BUT UP TILL CHRISTMAS WE HAD TO WALK SEVERAL MILES TO SCHOOL IN OUR FLOPPY SOLED SHOES OR GO BAREFOOT.

I REMEMBER WHEN I WAS IN THE FIRST GRADE POPPA AND MAMA HAD TO TAKE US OUT OF SCHOOL TO MOVE TO THE COTTON FIELDS SO WE COULD ALL PICK COTTON BECAUSE THEY NEEDED HELP OR PERHAPS IT WAS BECAUSE HE LOST HIS JOB AND THE ONLY ONE HE COULD FIND WAS PICKING COTTON, I DON'T RECALL WHICH. THEY DIDN'T HAVE MACHINES TO PICK COTTON, AT LEAST NOT THAT I KNEW OF AT THE TIME. WE PICKED COTTON BY HAND. POPPA TAUGHT US BOYS WORK ETHICS AND EXPECTED US TO PUT OUT EFFORT IN LIFE SO MY BROTHER AND I PICKED COTTON AND MY SISTERS HELP MAMA AROUND THE TENT HOUSE WE LIVED IN. MY OLDER BROTHERS WERE IN THE U. S. NAVY SO ONLY FOUR OF US KIDS WERE AT HOME. MY OLDER SISTER MARRIED THE ICE MAN WHEN SHE WAS SIXTEEN AND STARTED HER OWN FAMILY. HOWEVER, ALL OF US FLUNKED SCHOOL THAT YEAR BECAUSE OF MISSING SO MANY DAYS AND MONTHS. MY PARENTS DID THE BEST THEY COULD UNDER THE CIRCUMSTANCES. WE WERE BROKE – REALLY POOR, AS WERE MOST OF THE PEOPLE THAT WE KNEW.

WE DIDN'T EVEN KNOW ANYONE WHO HAD ELECTRICITY OR INSIDE TOILETS OR RUNNING WATER. WE USED COAL OIL LAMPS, AN OUTHOUSE (AT TIMES WE HAD A TWO HOLER – WHERE TWO PEOPLE COULD GO AT ONCE) AND WE DREW OUR WATER OUT OF A HOLE IN THE GROUND WITH A BUCKET ON A ROPE. WHILE WE LIVED IN THE TENT PICKING COTTON WE ATE PORK-N-BEANS THREE MEALS A DAY. WE DIDN'T HAVE AN ICE BOX SO THE PORK HAD TO BE SALTED TO PRESERVE IT – WOW WAS IT SALTY!

I REMEMBER THAT POPPA TOLD MY BROTHER AND I THAT HE WOULD GIVE A QUARTER (25 CENTS) TO THE FIRST ONE OF US THAT COULD PICK

100 POUNDS OF COTTON IN A DAY. FINALLY, AT CLOSE TO THE END OF COTTON PICKIN SEASON, I PICKED 101 POUNDS. WOW – A WHOLE QUARTER TO SPEND. I BOUGHT A POCKET KNIFE, AN OLD TIMER BY THE WAY, A COKE-A-COLA IN A BOTTLE, A CANDY BAR AND SOME CANDY FOR MY BROTHER AND SISTER WITH THAT ONE QUARTER. OH AND I GOT BACK 2 CENTS FOR THE EMPTY COKE-A-COLA BOTTLE WHICH WAS ENOUGH FOR SOME MORE CANDY.

I DECIDED SOMEWHERE IN THIS TIME PERIOD THAT I WANTED A LOT OF QUARTERS. THANK GOD FOR MY POPPA, MAMA AND MY OLDER BROTHER CHET WHO AT ABOUT 12 YEARS OLD GAVE ME A JOB IN CONSTRUCTION AND I WORKED HARD AND MADE THE SAME PAY AS THE MEN ON THE CONSTRUCTION JOBS. SO I QUIT SCHOOL AND WAS ON MY WAY TO MAKING A LIVING – THE WORKING MAN AND WOMANS WAY TO WEALTH!

BY THE TIME I WAS 17 I JOINED THE NAVY AND WAS TAUGHT MORE WORK ETHICS AND SELF DISCIPLINE. I STUDIED ELECTRONICS AND LEADERSHIP. THE NAVY MADE ME "TRAINING OFFICER" FOR THE BASE BY THE TIME I WAS 19 YEARS OLD AND I WASN'T EVEN AN OFFICER. UPON RELEASE THEY RECOMMENDED ME FOR OFFICERS CANDIDATE SCHOOL.

I WAS MARRIED AT 18 YEARS OLD, HAD A CHILD BY THE TIME I WAS 19 YEARS OLD, BOUGHT A HOUSE ON THE GI BILL AT 19 YEARS OLD, WAS STILL IN THE NAVY AND WORKED WEEK-ENDS OR WHEN EVER I COULD REPAIRING TV'S, ELECTRONICS, APPLICANCES OR ANYTHING ELECTRONIC OR ELECTRICAL THAT I COULD FIGURE OUT. THE NAVY DIDN'T PAY MUCH – MAYBE A DOLLAR AN HOUR – BUT LIVING EXPENSE WERE A LOT LESS AT THAT TIME. WIVES DIDN'T WORK IN THOSE DAYS. THEY TOOK CARE OF THE HOME AND KIDS. BUT THEY DIDN'T NEED TO EITHER IF THE HUSBAND WORKED HARD AND WE ALL DID. I WAS DETERMINED NOT TO BE POOR LIKE I HAD BEEN AS A CHILD. GOOD WORK ETHICS WILL ALWAYS GET YOU A JOB AND SELF DISCIPLINE WILL KEEP IT.

THERE WERE TIMES WHEN I HAVE DONE REALLY WELL AND MADE A LOT OF MONEY BUT DUE TO LACK OF AN EDUCATION THERE WERE ALSO TIMES THAT I MADE MISTAKES AND LOST ALL OF IT BUT WITH DETERMINATION AND GOOD WORK ETHICS I HAVE ALWAYS MADE A COME BACK, SO TO SPEAK.

SURE, A PERSON CAN THINK THEIRSELVES RICH IF THEY THINK OF HOW TO DO IT AND THEN PUT THAT THINKING IN MOTION THROUGH ACTION – WORK! I THOUGHT OF THIS BOOK BUT THINKING ABOUT IT WILL NOT MAKE ME WEALTHY – WORKING ON IT MIGHT. BELIEVE ME WRITING A BOOK IS WORK, TOO! IF MY MEMORY SERVES ME CORRECTLY, THIS IS ABOUT THE FIFTH TIME I HAVE RE-TYPED IT.

EVEN IDEAS TAKE WORK

REMEMBER WHAT WE WERE DISCUSSING EARLIER ABOUT LIVING BELOW YOUR MEANS AND SAVING THE EXTRA MONEY SO THAT YOU WILL BE ABLE TO TAKE ADVANTAGE OF OPPORTUNITIES THAT PRESENT THEMSELVES? CONSIDER THE FOLLOWING:

I READ SOMEWHERE THAT EVERYONE IS BLESSED WITH AN OPPORTUNITY TO BECOME MILLIONAIRES AT LEAST ONCE DURING THEIR LIFETIME. MOST PEOPLE PASS UP THAT OPPORTUNITY BECAUSE OF CIRCUMSTANCES OR, BECAUSE THEY DO NOT RECOGNIZE THE POTENTIAL OF THE OPPORTUNITY. OTHER TIMES WE PASS THEM UP BECAUSE IT'S OUR OWN IDEA AND WE DON'T TRUST OURSELVES ENOUGH TO BELIEVE IN SOMETHING THAT WE CAME UP WITH. SOMETIMES WE DISCUSS IT WITH OTHERS AND LATER FIND OUT THAT SOMEONE ELSE CAME UP WITH OUR IDEA AND IT IS NOW AVAILABLE TO THE PUBLIC.

LET ME SAY THIS: WHEN YOU HAVE AN IDEA FOLLOW THROUGH WITH IT, PUT IT ALL DOWN ON PAPER AND THEN IF IT ISN'T PERFECT TRY TO PERFECT IT IF YOU CAN. NECESSITY IS THE MOTHER OF INVENTENTION! IF YOU FOLLOW THROUGH ON AN IDEA, EVEN IF IT DOESN'T WORK OUT, DON'T QUIT! YOU HAVE STARTED YOUR CREATIVE JUICES FLOWING AND THE NEXT IDEA WILL BE BETTER AND THE NEXT ONE EVEN BETTER YET. EVEN THOMAS EDISON HAD FAILURES BUT HE DIDN'T QUIT! THE NEXT TIME HE HAD AN IDEA HE WORKED ON IT UNTIL IT BECAME SUCCESSFUL OR WAS THROWN IN THE TRASH.

WHAT I'M SAYING IS EVEN IDEAS TAKE WORK – EFFORT, TO MAKE THEM A REALITY. THERE IS NOT A LAZY WAY! YOU CAN BE AT THE RIGHT PLACE AT THE RIGHT TIME AND RECOGNIZE THE POTENTIAL OF AN OPPORTUNITY OR RECOGNIZE THE POTENTIAL OF YOUR OWN IDEA BUT YOU HAVE TO EXPEND SOME EFFORT AND HAVE SOME MONEY AVAILABLE TO MAKE IT A REALITY!

WHAT WILL HAPPEN IF?

EVERY TIME YOU DO ANYTHING YOU SHOULD STOP AND CONSIDER, "WHAT WILL HAPPEN IF?" WHAT WILL HAPPEN IF I DO THIS OR THAT? WHAT WILL HAPPEN IF I BUY THIS HOUSE OR WHAT WILL HAPPEN IF I DON'T? WHAT WILL HAPPEN IF I SELL MY HOME OR WHAT IF I DON'T?

REMEMBER THE HOME I BOUGHT WHEN I WAS 19 YEARS OLD? WELL I SOLD IT TO MY MOTHER FOR A SMALL PROFIT WHEN MY BROTHER AND I BOUGHT ANOTHER ONE AND STARTED REMODELING IT. SHE SOLD IT A COUPLE OF YEARS LATER AND MADE A PROFIT. I PASSED BY THAT HOUSE 23 YEARS LATER AND THERE WAS A FOR SALE SIGN UP SO I CALLED AND ASKED THE PRICE. THE OWNERS WERE ASKING $72,500.00 (1985) FOR THE HOUSE THAT I BOUGHT FOR $14,950.00 (1962) SOLD FOR $15,950.00 (1964) AND MY MOTHER SOLD FOR $22,500.00 (1966). WHAT'S IT WORTH IN 2007 - $400,000.00. SHOULD I HAVE CONSIDERED "WHAT WILL HAPPEN IF?"

ANOTHER TIME WHILE I WAS IN ALASKA I WAS INVOLVED IN A COUPLE OF BUSINESSES AND HAD STARTED A TIRE BUSINESS ALONG WITH A FRIEND NAMED BOB. WE HAD PUT IN A BID TO SUPPLY THE RUBBER FOR EVERY VEHICLE THAT WOULD BE WORKING ON THE UPCOMING TRANS ALASKAN PIPELINE CONSTRUCTION PROJECT. THE TIRE BUSINESS WASN'T GOING VERY WELL AND BOB DIDN'T HAVE ANY MORE MONEY TO PUT INTO IT SO I WAS SUPPORTING IT FROM MONEY I MADE WORKING MY OTHER BUSINESSES. WE DIDN'T THINK THAT WE SHOULD CONTINUE TO PUT MORE OF MY MONEY INTO IT SO WE CLOSED IT UP AND SOLD OUR TOOLS AND INVENTORY. I MOVED ON AND STARTED ANOTHER BUSINESS THAT, ALONG WITH THE ONES ALREADY GOING, CONSUMED THE REST OF MY TIME LEAVING ME JUST ENOUGH HOURS LEFT FOR SOME SLEEP. I WAS A WORKAHOLIC! A FEW MONTHS AFTER WE CLOSED THE TIRE BUSINESS ALEYESKA PIPELINE SERVICE COMPANY CALLED ME AND SAID THAT WE HAD THE CONTRACT WHICH I TURNED DOWN WITHOUT THINKING BECAUSE I WAS TOO BUSY ALREADY. WHAT A MISTAKE! THAT CONTRACT MADE THE COMPANY THAT TOOK IT MILLIONS. I SHOULD HAVE SAID LET ME CALL YOU BACK TOMORROW AND I SHOULD HAVE ASKED MYSELF "WHAT WILL HAPPEN IF?"!

SNAP DECISIONS ARE NOT ALWAYS THE BEST DECISIONS. LOOK OVER THE PROPERTY YOU ARE ABOUT TO BUY AND THINK ABOUT IT. ASK YOURSELF "WHAT WILL HAPPEN IF"!

INFLATION/APPRECIATION

THE RICH DON'T PAY INTEREST! DID YOU KNOW THAT?

THE RICH DO NOT WANT THE POOR PEOPLE TO BECOME WEALTHY! DO YOU KNOW THAT? IF THERE WERE NOT ANY POOR PEOPLE WHO WOULD DO ALL THE MANUAL LABOR? WHO WOULD FIX THEIR CAR, THEIR SINK WHEN IT PLUGGED UP, THEIR STREETS, THEIR ROOF WHEN IT LEAKED AND WHO WOULD MOW THEIR YARD OR CLEAN THEIR SWIMMING POOL? THINK ABOUT IT – THE ONLY THING THAT MAKES THEM RICH SO THEY CAN SWIM AND SOAK IN A HOT TUB ALL DAY IS MONEY. THE ONLY THING THAT MAKES THEM RICH IS BECAUSE THERE ARE POOR PEOPLE (MOST OF US). IF THERE WERE NO POOR THEN NO ONE WOULD BE RICH. THEY DON'T PAY INTEREST ON LOANS. THEY DON'T APPLY FOR PERSONAL LOANS; THEY JUST PAY CASH FOR IT OR PUT IT ON A CREDIT CARD THAT IS PAID IN FULL EACH MONTH WHICH MEANS THEY DON'T PAY INTEREST ON IT.

THE GOVERNMENT DOESN'T WANT YOU TO BECOME RICH, EITHER! DID YOU KNOW THAT?

THINK ABOUT THAT IDEA. WHY DON'T THEY WANT YOU RICH? BECAUSE IF EVERYONE IN AMERICA GOT WEALTHY ENOUGH TO RETIRE WHO DO YOU THINK WOULD DO ALL THE WORK FOR THE RICH? WHO WOULD COOK FOR THE PRESIDENT AND FIRST LADY AND CLEAN UP THEIR DIRTY BATHROOM? WHO WOULD WORK TO MAKE AN INCOME TO PAY THEIR BILLS AND TO PAY T A X E S ? HEY, TAXES ARE WHAT LET'S THE MILLIONS OF GOVERNMENT EMPLOYEES PAY THEIR BILLS AND ALLOWS MANY OF THEM LIVE LIKE ROYALTY! IF WE DIDN'T WORK AND PAY TAXES WHO WOULD PAY FOR ALL OF THAT?

SO, WHAT HAPPENED IS, THE RICH AND THE GOVERNMENT TOGETHER HAVE FIGURED OUT A WAY TO KEEP ALL OF US WORKING AND PAYING TAXES SO THEY CAN GET THEIR WORK DONE BY THE POOR AND SO THEY WILL BE ABLE TO CONTINUE LIVING LIKE ROYALTY.

NOT LONG AGO IT ONLY TOOK THE HUSBAND WORKING FOR A FAMILY TO LIVE AND PAY ALL THEIR BILLS EACH MONTH. SOME WIVES WOULD WORK SO THAT THE FAMILY COULD HAVE EXTRA SPENDING MONEY FOR THE TOYS WE ALL WANT BUT IN TIME MORE AND MORE WOMEN WERE DOING THAT AND SINCE THE GOVERNMENT AND THE RICH KEEP RECORDS THEY SOON REALIZED THAT A LOT OF FAMILIES WERE ACCUMULATING TOO MUCH MONEY AND WERE RETIREING EARLY.

SO HOW DO WE STOP THAT RUSH TOWARD WEALTH AND EARLY RETIREMENT? BREAK THE UNIONS (WHICH WERE MOSTLY MEN AT THAT

TIME) SO THAT THE PAY TO MEN WOULD DECREASE (READ SOME OF THE ARTICLES IN THIS BOOK – EMPLOYEES WERE TAKING PAY CUTS JUST TO KEEP A JOB). THEY DECIDED TO GIVE WOMEN EQUAL PAY FOR EQUAL WORK AND PUT ALL OF THEM TO WORK, TOO! BUT BY THE TIME THE SMOKE CLEARED WHATEVER SALARY THE MAN ALONE WAS MAKING WOULD NOW TAKE BOTH HUSBAND AND WIFE WORKING TO EQUAL THE SAME SALARY! WOW! THE FAMILY WAS NOW MAKING THE SAME PAY AS BEFORE BUT IT TOOK TWO PEOPLE WORKING TO EARN IT. WE ALLOWED THAT TO HAPPEN, DIDN'T WE? AND WHEN IT'S ALL SAID AND DONE WE'RE STILL BROKE AND WE ARE NOT GETTING WEALTHY, SO WE ARE FORCED TO CONTINUE TO DO THE DIRTY WORK FOR THE RICH AND PAY TAXES SO THAT THE GOVERNMENT CAN CONTINUE TO GROW BIGGER.

ANOTHER THING THEY DO IS CONTROL HOW WEALTHY YOU CAN GET BY CONTROLLING INFLATION/APPRECIATION! IF YOU BUY A HOME AND YOUR INTEREST ON THE MORTGAGE IS, LET'S SAY, 10% AND THE VALUE OF THE HOME IS GOING UP AT THE RATE OF 20% IT DOESN'T TAKE LONG FOR YOU TO MAKE A LOT OF MONEY JUST BY SELLING THE HOME. YOU COULD POSSIBLY RETIRE AND STOP PAYING TAXES. THEY CAN EVEN CONTROL HOW LONG IT TAKES US TO ACCUMULATE ENOUGH WEALTH TO RETIRE AND TO QUIT WORKING FOR THE RICH AND TO QUIT PAYING TAXES. THERE IS SOME "FALL OUT" TO THIS PLAN AND THEY KNOW IT. THERE WILL BE THOSE WHO LOSE THEIR JOB FOR SOME REASON AND LOSE THEIR CAR, LOSE THEIR HOME AND POSSIBLE EVERYTHING THEY OWN. THEY ARE WILLING TO LIVE WITH THIS "FALL OUT". AFTER ALL, THE MAJORITY IS ALL THEY CARE ABOUT AND GETTING THE WORK DONE AND COLLECTING TAXES.

NOW GUESS WHAT – EVERYTHING IN AMERICA TODAY IS MADE IN SOME OTHER COUNTRY! IT WON'T BE LONG AND THERE WILL NOT BE ANY JOBS LEFT FOR AMERICANS AND WHEN THAT HAPPENS WE WILL NOT BE ABLE TO SELL ANY MORE OF OUR TIME SO WE WILL NOT BE ABLE TO BECOME WEALTHY. IN FACT IF IT KEEPS UP WE MAY BECOME A THIRD WORLD COUNTRY!

THERE ARE TWO THINGS WE AS AMERICANS WHO LOVE OUR COUNTRY AND OUR LIFESTYLE CAN DO. WE CAN IMMEDIATELY STOP BUYING ANYTHING THAT SAYS MADE IN: (ANYWHERE EXCEPT THE USA). A LOT OF OUR MONEY IS ACTUALLY GOING TO OUR ENEMIES – A COUNTRY THAT DOESN'T LIKE AMERICANS OR CHRISTIANS (CHRISTIANITY IS THE MAJORITY BELIEF IN AMERICA).

AND THE SECOND THING WE CAN DO IS THIS: IF WE WANT TO GO BACK TO THE DAYS WHEN ONLY ONE PERSON HAD TO WORK TO SUPPORT THE FAMILY WHICH ALLOWED US TO GIVE GUIDANCE TO OUR KIDS BECAUSE ONE OF US WAS ALWAYS WATCHING THEM - THEN SOMEONE HAS TO QUIT

THEIR JOB! I DON'T CARE WHICH ONE – BUT ONE MUST DO IT! IF WE WANT TO BECOME A NATION OF HOUSE-HUSBANDS THEN GUYS QUIT YOUR JOB AND LET YOUR WIFE SUPPORT THE FAMILY. LIVE WITHIN THE BUDGET OF HER INCOME ALONE. DOWN SIZE! OF COURSE, IF WE PREFER FOR THE WOMAN TO RAISE THE KIDS, THEN LADIES YOU ALL NEED TO QUIT YOUR JOB AND LET YOUR HUSBAND SUPPORT THE FAMILY. PERSONALLY I BELIEVE WOMEN DO A MUCH BETTER JOB OF RAISING KIDS WITH SELF CONTROL, RESPECT FOR OTHERS, LOVE AND KINDNESS THAN THE MEN DO. THAT'S JUST MY PERSONAL OPINION AND I DO BELIEVE THAT WOMEN SHOULD RUN THE HOME AND MOST DECISIONS SHOULD BE SHARED EQUALLY WITH HER HUSBAND AND HIS DECISIONS SHOULD BE MADE EQUALLY WITH HIS WIFE.

TO GO BACK TO THOSE DAYS WILL TAKE A GRASS ROOTS EFFORT AND PATIENCE BUT IN TIME THE ONE WORKING PARTNERS SALARY WILL GET BACK TO WHERE IT SHOULD BE. WHY WOULD IT? BECAUSE WE AS A FAMILY WILL NOT BE PAYING AS MUCH TAXES AS WE ARE NOW AND BECAUSE WE WON'T BE BUYING THE RICH MANS PRODUCTS. WITH PATIENCE, AND AFTER THE SMOKE CLEARS, THE PARTNER THAT ISN'T WORKING CAN SPEND THE TIME KIDS NEED TEACHING THEM RESPECT AND VALUES. THEN LATER, IF THEY WANT TO, THEY CAN GET A PART TIME JOB SO THAT THEY CAN AFFORD THOSE EXTRAS WE ALL WANT.

I RECALL WHEN I WAS YOUNGER THAT AMERICANS WERE THE WEALTHY PEOPLE AROUND THE WORLD AND WE WERE ON THE SALARY OF JUST ONE WORKING FAMILY MEMBER – NOT TWO. ALL OF THE OTHER COUNTRIES LOVED US – WE WERE THERE SPENDING MONEY AND OUR GOVERNMENT STAYED OUT OF THEIR BUSINESS AND WASN'T CONTROLING THEM. MANY OF THEM TODAY DO NOT EVEN LIKE AMERICANS AND THEY WANT OUR GOVERNMENT TO STAY OUT OF THEIR BUSINESS. IF WE HAD NEVER GOT STARTED WITH NOSEING INTO THEIR BUSINESS WE PROBABLY WOULD NOT HAVE A 13 TRILLION DOLLAR DEBT.

OUR ECONOMY IS ALLOWED TO HAVE A SMALL AMOUNT OF INFLATION EVERY YEAR AND BECAUSE OF THAT INFLATION OUR HOMES AND LAND DO APPRECIATE IN VALUE BUT GENERALLY NOT ENOUGH TO PAY THE COST OF INTEREST WE ARE PAYING ON THE LOANS. IF APPRECIATION IS ONLY 4% AND WE ARE PAYING SOMEWHERE BETWEEN 8% AND 36% INTEREST WE ARE LOSEING MONEY OVER THE LONG HAUL.

EVER ONCE IN A WHILE THE PEOPLE ACTUALLY BY ACCIDENT MAKE THINGS HAPPEN THAT ALLOWS US TO GROW FINANCIALLY IN LEAPS AND BOUNDS – THEN THEY GET CONTROL OF IT AGAIN.

THE PROSPEROUS PERIOD

AS YOU SEE BY THE ABOVE, INFATION STEADILY INCREASES THE VALUE OF A HOME AND PUTS MONEY IN YOUR POCKET WHEN YOU SELL IT AT THE NEW VALUE 20 – 30 – 40 OR MORE YEARS AFTER YOU PURCHASED IT. THERE IS A DOWNSIDE TO THIS THOUGH. IF YOU SELL IT AT THE NEW VALUE WHERE ARE YOU GOING TO MOVE TO? WHERE WILL YOU LIVE ONCE IT IS SOLD? ANOTHER HOME THAT COMPARES TO YOUR HOME WILL COST YOU ABOUT THE SAME AS WHAT YOU JUST SOLD YOUR HOME FOR SO ALL YOU ARE DOING IS TRADING HOMES.

A LADY I HAVE KNOWN FOR 20 YEARS JUST RECENTLY RECEIVED AN OFFER FOR HER HOME WHICH WAS ON TWO AND ONE HALF ACRES NEAR MARICOPA ARIZONA. IT WAS A NICE PLACE WITH FOUR BEDROOMS, A LOT OF LAND, SEVERAL OUT BUILDINGS FOR STORAGE AND SHOPS AND MORE WHICH SHE OWNED AFTER HER HUSBAND PASSED AWAY. WHEN SHE ASKED ME WHAT I THOUGHT, I REPLIED, "IF YOU SELL OUT, WHERE WILL YOU MOVE TO? ANY PLACE WILL COST YOU AS MUCH OR MORE THAN YOU SELL YOUR HOME FOR!" SHE EXPLAINED THAT SHE WANTED CLOSER TO DOWNTOWN AND CLOSER TO THE DOCTORS OFFICE. WITH THAT IN MIND SHE SHOULD PROBABLY SELL AND MOVE – NOT BECAUSE OF THE MONEY. SHE ENDED UP FINDING A MANUFACTURED HOME IN A PARK THAT SHE COULD BUY WHICH WAS A LOT CLOSER TO HER DOCTOR AND SHE SOLD HER HOME OF OVER 20 YEARS AND MOVED. IT WORKED OUT BECAUSE OF THE BENEFITS SHE RECEIVED IN THE TRANSACTION THAT WERE IMPORTANT TO HER.

DURING THE PROSPEROUS PERIOD FROM THE 50'S THROUGH THE 90'S, THOUGH THERE WERE SOME UPS AND DOWNS, ANYONE WHO OWNED A HOME MADE GOOD MONEY FROM INFLATION AND YOU CAN STILL TAKE ADVANTAGE OF THIS.

WHEN I BOUGHT MY FIRST HOME IN 1962 THE PAYMENTS WITH INTEREST, TAXES AND INSURANCE WAS ONLY $121.00 A MONTH. IF I HAD KNOWN WHAT I KNOW NOW I WOULD HAVE BOUGHT ANOTHER ONE AND RENTED IT OUT. WHAT WOULD HAVE HAPPENED IF I HAD BOUGHT TWO OR MORE RENTALS? I COULD HAVE AFFORDED THE PAYMENTS ON THE SECOND HOUSE BECAUSE I WAS SELLING A LOT OF TIME! I WAS WORKING 12 HOURS A DAY SIX DAYS A WEEK! IN ADDITION, I COULD HAVE RENTED IT OUT FOR $125.00 A MONTH AND RENTERS WOULD HAVE PAID IT OFF FOR ME. BUT I WAS TOO BUSY WORKING AND ENJOYING WHAT I HAD AND THE MONEY I WAS MAKING, SO I DIDN'T STOP TO THINK ABOUT THAT.

IF YOU OWN YOUR OWN HOME AND MAYBE SOME LAND BEFORE A PROSPEROUS SURGE YOU CAN MAKE A LOT OF MONEY.

CAN WE AFFORD A HOME TODAY?

(1985) LET ME QUOTE SOME OF THE DEC. 1982 READER'S DIGEST ARTICLE ON "NEW WAYS TO BUY AND SELL HOUSES".
IN THE ARTICLE, MR. AND MRS. BROWN WERE TRYING TO FIND A HOME THAT THEY COULD AFFORD ON HIS $25,000.00 SALARY. THEY FINALLY FOUND ONE FOR $73,600.00 BUT COULD NOT AFFORD IT WITHOUT BORROWING MONEY FROM RELATIVES. MR. BROWN SAYS, "HOW CAN THE AVERAGE FAMILY AFFORD A HOME TODAY?"
THE ARTICLE GOES ON TO SAY, "IS A HOME OF ONE'S OWN – LONG WITHIN REACH OF MOST WAGE EARNERS – BECOMING AMERICA'S IMPOSSIBLE DREAM? LONG-TERM MORTGAGES AT INTEREST RATES BELOW TEN PERCENT, THE FOUNDATION OF THE POSTWAR HOUSING BOOM, HAVE VANISHED." AND, RICHARD W. WIRTH, VICE PRESIDENT OF HOMEEQUITY, INC. SAYS, IN THE ARTICLE, "IT'S THE WORST HOUSING MESS SINCE THE GREAT DEPRESSION".
THE ARTICLE GOES ON TO SAY THAT THERE'S A NEW ART IN BUYING AND SELLING HOUSES AND:
"HERE'S WHAT THE NEW GROUND RULES MEAN:
"FIRST-HOME SHOPPERS WILL NEED TO LOWER THEIR EXPECTATIONS, SETTLING FOR LESS IN ORDER TO GET ON THE HOUSING ESCALATOR.
"UNLIKE YESTERDAYS FIXED-RATE MORTGAGES, FLEXIBLE MORTGAGES USUALLY CAN BE REFINANCED WITHOUT COSTLY FEES OR PENALTIES….."
"BECAUSE MORTGAGES WILL BE MORE EXPENSIVE, MANY NEW HOMES WILL BE SMALLER – AND EITHER ATTACHED OR RANDOMLY PLACED, WITH AS MANY AS A DOZEN TO THE ACRE."
THE ARTICLE SUGGESTS BUYING MOBILE HOMES OR RENOVATING SLUM HOUSES.

(1985) ANOTHER ARTICLE IN READER'S DIGEST, JULY 1983 IS ENTITLED "BRAVO FOR OLD BUILDINGS!". IT TALKS ABOUT OLDER HISTORIC BUILDINGS AND IT SAYS THAT HOUSES IN CAPE MAY, N. J. WHICH WERE SELLING FOR $20,000.00 IN 1970 ARE NOW BRINGING $150,000.00. WHY? BECAUSE PEOPLE ARE FIXING UP THE OLD HOUSES AND RESTORING THEM. ALSO, THE AVERAGE PRICE OF NEW HOMES ARE UP AROUND $140,000.00 OR MORE, IN SOME STATES.

(1985) MOST OF US HAVEN'T JUMPED ABOARD THIS "HOUSING ESCALATOR" IDEA YET BECAUSE WE DON'T RECOGNIZE ITS POTENTIAL. WE ARE STILL GOING OUT AND BUYING NEW HOMES FOR $100,000.00 OR MORE. WE'RE STILL PAYING MORE THAN WE CAN AFFORD. WE'RE BUYING LARGE NEW HOMES WITH LONG TERM MORTGAGES AND HIGH INTEREST RATES. WE'RE BUYING WHAT WE WANT NOT WHAT WE REALLY CAN AFFORD. ARE WE TRYING TO IMPRESS OUR FRIENDS AND RELATIVES?

WELL, THAT IS PART OF THE PROBLEM! WE ALL LOOK LIKE WE'RE DOING GREAT BUT MOST OF US END UP LIVING ON SOCIAL SECURITY AND MEAGER INCOMES. WHY? BECAUSE WE'VE SPENT ALL OUR HARD EARNED MONEY PAYING INTEREST FOR 30 YEARS OR MORE. WE THOUGHT THAT BUYING A HOME WOULD MAKE US MONEY – BUT IT DIDN'T. WE PAID MORE INTEREST THAN IT APPRECIATED AND AFTER ALL THOSE YEARS OF PAYMENTS SOME PEOPLE LOSE THEIR HOMES AND OTHERS CAN'T SELL BECAUSE THE COST TO FIND A REPLACEMENT HOME WOULD BE THE SAME AS THE ONE WE JUST SOLD, OR MORE, SO WE LEAVE IT IN OUR WILL TO SOMEONE WHO WILL BENEFIT FROM OUR YEARS OF DOING WITHOUT.

DURING THE WORKING LIFETIME OF MOST AMERICANS WE MAY LOOK LIKE WE ARE WEALTHY BUT WE'RE NOT: WE HAVE A NICE HOME, NICE FURNITURE AND OF COURSE TWO NEW CARS. WE LOOK WEALTHY, RIGHT? WE JUST LOOK THAT WAY! WE OWE LARGE DEBTS ON OUR HOME, CAR PAYMENTS, FURNITURE PAYMENTS AND MORE – AND, WE WILL MOST LIKELY PAY ON THOSE FOR OUR ENTIRE LIFETIME. LET ME ASK YOU THIS: WHICH IS BETTER (1) TO LOOK WEALTHY, OR, (2) TO BE WEALTHY?

I WILL SAY THIS ABOUT THE MARKET RIGHT NOW – AT THE TIME I AM RE-WRITING THIS BOOK – IN MY AREA, WHICH IS NEAR PHOENIX ARIZONA, IT IS A BUYERS MARKET. FOR FIVE YEARS WE WENT THROUGH A HUGE INCREASE IN LAND VALUES BUT JUST LAST YEAR WE STARTED A DOWN TURN BUT I PERSONALLY DON'T BELIEVE IT IS GOING MUCH LOWER. THERE ARE PEOPLE TODAY WHO BOUGHT WHEN THE PRICES WERE AT THEIR HIGEST - ON CREDIT- AND ARE NOW STRUGGLING TO PAY THE PAYMENTS. MANY OTHERS BOUGHT ON A PAYMENT PLAN WHERE THEY PAY LOW INTEREST FOR THREE OR FOUR YEARS AND AT THE END OF THAT TIME THE PAYMENTS WILL JUMP UP TO A NORMAL RATE. THEY ARE TRYING TO GET OUT OF THOSE BAD DEALS BEFORE THEY END UP LOSING WHAT THEY BOUGHT, THEIR DOWN PAYMENTS AND THE PAYMENTS THEY HAVE MADE. SOME OF THE LAND THAT WAS SELLING IN THIS AREA FOR 60K AN ACRE TWO OR THREE YEARS AGO IS NOW BRINGING 30K AN ACRE SO I HAVE BOUGHT SOME MORE BECAUSE THE HUGE HOUSING AND COMMERCIAL DEVELOPMENTS ARE HEADING TOWARD IT.

YOU MIGHT WANT TO CONSIDER LOOKING AROUND FOR SOMETHING DURING DOWN SWINGS IN THE MARKET.

WHILE YOU ARE LOOKING BE CERTAIN TO KEEP IN MIND EVERYTHING THAT YOU HAVE READ IN THIS BOOK AND BUY SOMETHING WITH POTENTIAL THAT YOU CAN AFFORD AND ONE THAT WILL LEAVE MONEY IN YOUR POCKET AFTER BILLS ARE PAID EVERY PAYDAY.

IF THE WHOLE WORLD WAS COVERED WITH LAND WOULD IT ALL BE MORTGAGED?

ABSOLUTELY! THE RICH WANT TO STAY RICH AND THEY WANT TO KEEP EVERYONE ELSE BROKE! THEY CAN DO THAT BY KEEPING US IN DEBT FOREVER. THE GOVERNMENT CAN'T ALLOW ALL OF US TO BECOME WEALTHY EITHER! IF WE WERE – WHO WOULD DO THE WORK? IF WE DIDN'T WORK WE WOULDN'T HAVE AN INCOME – WHO WOULD PAY TAXES? THEY PROVED THAT WHEN THEY BROKE THE AIR TRAFFIC CONTROLLERS UNION AND MORE! THE AIR TRAFFIC CONTROLLERS UNION WAS DEMANDING PAY EQUAL TO THE 747 PILOTS WAGES WHICH WOULD MAKE THEM WEALTHY IN A SHORT TIME AND THAT JUST COULDN'T HAPPEN. WHEN I WAS A KID THE MAN WORKED AND THE WOMAN STAYED HOME AND TOOK CARE OF THE HOME AND KIDS. I'M NOT SAYING THAT WOMEN SHOULDN'T GET EQUAL PAY OR THAT THEY SHOULD STAY HOME! I'M JUST STATING A FACT! ON JUST THE MANS PAY THE FAMILY HAD A HOME, TWO CARS, COULD TAKE A VACATION EVERY YEAR, PAY THE BILLS AND SEND THE KIDS TO COLLEGE. TODAY IT TAKES BOTH THE HUSBAND AND WIFE WORKING JUST TO SURVIVE.

DOES EVERYONE YOU KNOW PAY HOUSE PAYMENTS OR RENT THEIR HOUSE? ALMOST EVERYONE I KNOW OR TALK TO EITHER RENTS OR PAYS HOUSE PAYMENTS! RENTING IS A WASTE BECAUSE IT ALL GOES TO SOMEONE ELSE – EVERY PENNY YOU PAY IS WASTED! SOMETIMES BUYING A HOUSE IS A WASTE BUT IF YOU BUY THE CORRECT HOUSE, AS WE ARE DISCUSSING, YOU WILL ACTUALLY MAKE MONEY FROM THE INVESTMENT – SOMETIMES A LOT OF MONEY! YOU CAN GET WEALTHY!

ASK YOURSELF SOME SERIOUS QUESTIONS: DO I THROW AWAY MY MONEY ON RENT OR, ON A BAD INVESTMENT IN THE WRONG HOUSE? DO I HAVE ANY MONEY LEFT EACH MONTH FOR EMERGENCIES; TO SPEND ON THE LITTLE EXTRAS LIKE A NEW COAT, NEW CAR AND DINNER IN A NICE RESTAURANT, ETC? DO I HAVE SOME CASH BUILT UP FOR URGENT NEEDS?

ASK YOURSELF: HAVE I PAID HOUSE PAYMENTS FOR TEN YEARS NOW AND DO I STILL OWE PAYMENTS FOR ANOTHER TEN OR TWENTY YEARS?

MOST OF THE LAND THAT WE THE PEOPLE OWN IS MORTGAGED! WELL, EXCEPT FOR MINE! AND, OF COURSE, EXCEPT FOR THE LAND THAT THE RICH OWN. IF THE RICH COULD THEY WOULD MORTGAGE THE ENTIRE EARTH.

ARE YOU BROKE?

DO YOU KNOW WHAT BROKE IT? ARE YOU BROKE? WELL, IF YOU'RE LIKE MOST AMERICANS (AND I HOPE YOU'RE NOT) YOU'RE BROKE! HOW CAN I SAY THAT? AMERICA IS THE LAND OF THE WEALTHY (SO WE ARE TOLD)! LET ME ASK A FEW QUESTIONS AND YOU WILL SEE IF YOU'RE BROKE OR NOT. IF YOU WERE SUDDENLY OUT OF A JOB WITH NO INCOME FOR THREE MONTHS WOULD YOU GET BEHIND ON YOUR BILLS? IF YOU WERE WITHOUT WORK FOR SIX MONTHS WOULD YOU LOSE YOUR CAR? WOULD YOU LOSE BOTH CARS? IF YOU DIDN'T HAVE ANY INCOME FOR NINE MONTHS OR EVEN FOR A YEAR WOULD YOU LOSE YOUR HOUSE? IF YOU'RE LIKE MOST AMERICANS YOU WOULD HAVE TO ANSWER YES TO THESE QUESTIONS.IF YOUR ANSWER IS YES – YOU ARE BROKE!

IF YOU ARE LIKE A LOT OF AMERICANS AND I'M ONE OF THEM, YOU'VE HAD A LOT MORE AT TIMES THAN YOU HAVE RIGHT NOW. AT ONE TIME, NOT TOO AWFULLY LONG AGO, I HAD THREE BUSINESSES, OWNED MY OWN HOME, HAD ANOTHER ONE SOLD AND IN ESCROW, HAD RENTAL UNITS AND MORE BUT BECAUSE OF SOME INVESTMENT MISTAKES I LOST THOSE THINGS. I LEARNED SOME LESSONS FROM THOSE LOSES AND BECAUSE OF WHAT I LEARNED, WHICH IS THE LESSONS I AM WRITING IN THIS BOOK, I WAS ABLE TO MAKE A COME BACK. LET ME GIVE YOU SOME ADVICE RIGHT NOW: DON'T EVER PUT YOUR HOME AT RISK. GO TO THE STATIONARY STORE AND GET A HOMESTEAD FORM AND FILE A HOMESTEAD ON YOUR HOME WHICH PROTECTS IT FROM DEBTS OWED!

IN 1985 I HEARD ON THE NEWS THAT AMERICA HAD MORE BANK FAILURES THAN WE'VE HAD SINCE THE 30'S. PEOPLE WITH MASTERS DEGREES WERE WASHING DISHES AND SELLING USED CARS; WORKERS WERE TAKING PAY-CUTS TO KEEP THEIR JOBS. KEEP IN MIND, THIS COULD HAPPEN AGAIN, ANY TIME.

WE MAY STILL HAVE TO FIND A JOB WASHING DISHES OR SELLING USED CARS IF WE LOSE OUR JOB EVEN WITH THE INFORMATION THAT YOU LEARN FROM THIS BOOK BUT WE SHOULDN'T LOSE OUR HOME AND BE BROKE!

THE AMERICAN DREAM

BUYING A HOME IS THE BIGGEST INVESTMENT MOST FAMILIES MAKE IN THEIR LIFETIME! AND IT'S USUALLY AN INVESTMENT THAT IS BREAK EVEN AT BEST. HOWEVER, IF IT IS DONE PROPERLY IT WOULD AND SHOULD BE A GOOD INVESTMENT AND COULD BECOME WHAT MAKES YOU WEALTHY.

RENTING IS A BIG WASTE OF MONEY BECAUSE WHAT WE PAY OUT IS ALL WASTED! YOU PAY IT OUT, THE RICH GET RICHER AND YOU STAY BROKE!

SO, WHAT DO WE DO? WHERE DO WE LIVE?

FIRST, LET ME SAY THIS. I AM NOT SAYING THAT BUYING A HOME IS WHAT KEEPS AMERICANS BROKE; USUALLY IT IS A COMBINATION OF THINGS. WHAT I AM SAYING IS THAT A HOME IS THE AMERICAN DREAM, IT'S SOMETHING WE ALL WANT AND SOMETHING WE PURSUE, IF WE ARE PRUDENT. HOWEVER, ONCE MANY PEOPLE HAVE GOTTEN THERE HOME IT BECOMES A BURDEN! A HOME SHOULD BE SOMETHING WE ENJOY, NOT A HEADACHE AND IF WE TAKE THE RIGHT APPROACH TO A HOME WE CAN ENJOY IT AND KEEP IT – EVEN IN HARD TIMES.

IF YOU BUY THE RIGHT HOME, AT THE RIGHT PRICE, WITH THE RIGHT TERMS, PERHAPS ONE OF YOU – THE HOUSE-HUSBAND OR THE HOUSE-WIFE – CAN BE JUST THAT AND STAY HOME AND YOUR FAMILY WON'T NEED THE EXTRA INCOME. IF THE ONE THAT DOESN'T WORK DECIDES TO GO TO WORK IT WILL BE JUST FOR EXTRA MONEY WHICH CAN BE USED TO MAKE MORE MONEY OR FOR THE TOYS WE ALL WANT.

(1985). KEEP IN MIND – WHAT HAPPENED YEARS AGO CAN REPEAT ITSELF AND IT DOES. MONEY MAGAZINE (DEC. 1985) SAYS IN AN ARTICLE UNDER BORROWING, "THE NEW PERILS OF DEBT – TAKING ON LOANS USED TO BE SMART. NOW YOU SHOULD RESIST THE CREDIT CELEBRITIES' SIREN SONG." AND, IN THE ARTICLE – "SOME HOMEOWNERS……ARE MAILING THEIR HOUSE KEYS BACK TO LENDERS." THIS ARTICLE SAYS A LOT TO ME – WE ARE THERE AGAIN IN 2007! READ THE NEWS ABOUT THE HOUSING MARKET IN AMERICA TODAY. IT IS BAD! BUT MY PERSONAL EXPECTATIONS ARE THAT IT WILL START BACK UP LATE THIS YEAR OR EARLY NEXT YEAR. NO GUARANTEES THOUGH!

TIP: IF YOU ARE GOING TO BUY A HOME IN THE NEAR FUTURE YOU SHOULD CONSIDER LOOKING AROUND NOW AND NEGOTIATE BECAUSE SELLERS WANT TO SELL RIGHT NOW. IT'S CALLED A BUYERS MARKET AND IN REALITY YOU CAN REALLY GET SOME GOOD DEALS WHEN THAT OCCURS. PLEASE READ THE REST OF THIS BOOK AND DON'T OVER

EXTEND YOURSELF WITH PAYMENTS YOU CAN'T AFORD. LIVE BELOW YOUR MEANS FOR A LITTLE WHILE, PRACTICE WHAT YOU ARE READING AND SOON YOU WILL HAVE THE AMERICAN DREAM FOR YOURSELF.

RENTERS THROW AWAY THOUSANDS OF DOLLARS A YEAR

RENTING IS A LOT WORSE THAN BUYING ALMOST ANY HOME WITHIN YOUR BUDGET AND ONE THAT FITS YOUR NEEDS! EVERY TIME YOU GIVE YOUR LANDLORD A RENT CHECK YOU'RE JUST THROWING AWAY HARD EARNED MONEY. YOU'RE NOT BUILDING ANY EQUITY IN THE RENTED HOUSE OR APARTMENT.

MOST YOUNG COUPLES AND FAMILIES CAN'T AFFORD TO BUY A HOME BY THE USUAL APPROACH TO FINANCING AND ESPECIALLY IF THEY BUY A NEW ONE. THERE IS GOOD NEWS – THEY DON'T HAVE TO RENT!

DO YOU REALIZE THAT THE COST TO MOVE INTO A RENTAL SOMETIMES WILL COST AS MUCH AS IT WOULD COST TO BUY A HOUSE, IF YOU LOOK FOR THE RIGHT HOUSE AND THEY ARE OUT THERE WAITING FOR A BUYER. IF YOU PAY $800.00 A MONTH FOR RENT THAT AMOUNTS UP TO $9,600.00 A YEAR WHICH IS $96,000.00 IN ONLY TEN YEARS. ADD THAT AMOUNT UP FOR 40 YEARS AND SEE WHAT YOU HAVE WASTED.

I MUST ASK THIS QUESTION AGAIN: WOULD YOU PREFER TO LOOK LIKE YOU ARE DOING GOOD OR WOULD YOU PREFER TO ACTUALLY BE WEALTHY? TO ACTUALLY BE WEALTHY TAKES A LITTLE TIME AND WORK BUT IT DOESN'T TAKE NEARLY AS LONG AS YOU MIGHT THINK – IF YOU DO IT THE RIGHT WAY.

OH YES – THANK YOU.

I WOULD LIKE TO THANK YOU FOR BUYING MY BOOK AND IF YOU CAN LEARN TO DO WITH A LITTLE LESS THAN WHAT YOU REALLY WANT YOU CAN DO THE SAME THING THAT I HAVE DONE. I REALLY WANT TO THANK MY MOTHER AND FATHER FOR GIVING ME DISCIPLINE AND WORK ETHICS. I REALLY WANT TO THANK MY BROTHER CHET FOR LETTING ME GET EXPERIENCE IN MANY FIELDS THAT WOULD HELP ME THROUGHOUT MY LIFE TO BE SUCCESSFUL. I REALLY WANT TO THANK MY BROTHER TED AND ALL OF MY FRIENDS THROUGH THE YEARS THAT DIDN'T MIND HELPING ME WHEN I NEEDED HELP. SOME WOULD SAY, WHEN I ASKED IF THEY COULD GIVE ME A HAND ON SOMETHING, "THAT SOUNDS LIKE A SIX PACKER", MEANING THAT IF I BOUGHT A SIX PACK OF BEER THAT THEY WOULD COME HELP. THANK YOU AND MAY GOD BLESS YOU.

LET ME SAY THIS BEFORE I GO TO THE NEXT CHAPTER. EVERYONE YOU ARE RELATED TO AND ALL YOUR FRIENDS (AND THEIR FRIENDS) ARE MORE THAN WILLING TO HELP YOU SUCCEED. IF ONE OF THEM IS A CARPENTER ASK FOR HELP; IF ONE OF THEM IS A PLUMBER ASK FOR HELP; IF ONE OF THEM KNOWS SOMEONE WHO CAN HELP WITH CARPET ASK WHO IT IS AND TALK TO THEM, AND; BE WILLING TO PAY THE ONES THAT NEED OR ASK TO BE PAID AND BE GRACIOUS TO THOSE WHO DO IT OUT OF FRIENDSHIP – BUT BE WILLING TO RETURN THE FAVOR. REMEMBER, IF YOU WANT A FRIEND YOU HAVE TO BE A FRIEND!

HOORAY FOR OLDER HOMES

THERE HAVE BEEN A FEW TIMES IN MY LIFE THAT I HAVE ACTUALLY FOUND IT NECESSARY TO RENT A HOUSE RATHER THAN BUYING ONE AND I ACCEPTED THAT FACT BUT I WAS ALWAYS ON THE LOOKOUT FOR A BUYABLE HOUSE WHEN AND IF I HAD TIME TO LOOK, AFTER SELLING TWELVE TO SIXTEEN HOURS A DAY OF MY TIME. ONCE, WHILE LIVING IN FAIRBANKS ALASKA AND RENTING, THE OWNER OF THE HOUSE KNOCKED ON THE DOOR AND SAID THAT WE SHOULD MOVE WITHIN 30 DAYS BECAUSE HE HAD MOVED BACK TO THE STATE AND WANTED TO MOVE BACK INTO HIS HOME. IT WAS THE FIRST OF MARCH AND THE TEMPERATURE WAS STILL AS COLD AS MINUS 40 DEGREES AT TIMES. WHAT A SURPRISE! I KNEW IT WAS GOING TO BE HARD TO FIND A HOUSE AT THAT TIME OF YEAR IN FAIRBANKS BUT I DIDN'T GET AN AGREEMENT WITH HIM THAT WOULD ALLOW ME TO STAY UNTIL SPRING (MY MISTAKE) SO NOW I NEEDED TO FIND A HOUSE FOR MY FAMILY WITHIN A MONTH.

AFTER WORK, EVERY DAY, I WOULD SPEND TIME LOOKING FOR A HOUSE TO RENT OR BUY BUT I COULDN'T FIND ONE. I DID HOWEVER FIND FIVE ACRES AROUND TEN MILES FROM TOWN AND ON BADGER ROAD. BADGER ROAD WAS PAVED AND THERE WAS A SIDE ROAD ALONG THE EAST SIDE OF THE FIVE ACRES FOR ACCESS FROM BADGER ROAD. THE LAND HAD AN OLD LOG HOUSE ON IT THAT WAS BUILD IN 1903 BUT IT DIDN'T HAVE ELECTRIC TO THE HOUSE NOR DID IT HAVE WATER, SEWAGE, WINDOWS IN THE HOLES FOR THEM, DOORS ON THE FRONT OR BACK AND THERE WAS ONE INCH CRACKS BETWEEN THE LOGS. WE COULD BE ANYWHERE IN THE HOUSE AND STILL SEE OUTSIDE THROUGH THE CRACKS BETWEEN THE LOGS. IT WAS UNINHABITABLE BY MOST PEOPLES STANDARDS (WOULD IT BE FOR YOU?) AND WAS BARELY SO BY MINE.

THE ONLY REASON IT WAS HABITABLE BY MY STANDARDS IS BECAUSE THE WINTERS IN FAIRBANKS ARE EIGHT TO NINE MONTHS LONG AND IF ONE DOESN'T GET OUT AND ENJOY THEM YOU WILL BECOME HOMEBOUND AND GET WHAT THEY CALL CABIN FEVER WHERE YOU NEVER WANT TO LEAVE HOME FOR ANY REASON. I WOULD TAKE MY FAMILY ON CAMPING TRIPS AND LIVE IN A TENT FOR THREE OR FOUR DAYS EVEN WHEN IT WAS TWENTY BELOW ZERO (ONE TIME IT DROPPED TO 40 BELOW ZERO), WHEN I COULD GET THE TIME OFF WORK. EVERYONE I KNEW WOULD DO THE SAME THING, AFTER ALL THAT IS PART OF WHY WE WANTED TO LIVE IN ALASKA IN THE FIRST PLACE AND WE ALL LOVED IT. I HAD TAUGHT MY WIFE AT THE TIME AND OUR THREE KIDS ALL ABOUT HOW TO BE PREPARED FOR ANY SITUATION IN THE COLD AND HOW TO DEAL WITH ANIMALS AND OTHER SITUATIONS. WE HAD CAMPED AND DEALT WITH LIVING OFF OF THE LAND DURING THE WINTER MANY

TIMES. SOMETIMES A FRIEND OR MY BROTHER TED AND I WOULD GO ON TRIPS BY MOUNT MCKINLEY OR MOUNT BLACKBURN AND OTHER DESTINATIONS BY FOOT OR BY MOTOR BIKE OR BY DOG SLED FOR UP TO TWO WEEKS AT A TIME AND LIVE OFF OF THE LAND. I WAS A PILOT SO WE WOULD SOMETIMES LAND AT LOCATIONS IN THE BROOKS MOUNTAIN RANGE WHERE THERE WASN'T ANY RUNWAYS AND STAY FOR DAYS. BEING PREPARED FOR THE WORST IS THE KEY TO SURVIVAL. I HAVE A LOT OF STORIES ABOUT THAT BUT I GUESS THAT IS ANOTHER BOOK.

IN ANY CASE, BACK TO THE HOUSE, WE DECIDED THAT WE COULD LIVE THERE AND FIX IT UP AND THAT WE WOULDN'T BE WASTING OUR MONEY ON RENT – IT WOULD BE OURS AND WE WOULDN'T BE SURPRISED BY A LANDLORD AGAIN! THE OWNER SOLD IT TO US FOR A REASONABLE DOWN PAYMENT AND CARRIED THE MORTGAGE HIMSELF WITH A CONTRACT OF SALE. I DIDN'T KNOW MUCH ABOUT THE LEGALITIES OF THAT AT THE TIME BUT HE WAS HONEST AND LATER WHEN I PAID IT OFF HE COMPLETED THE SALE AND IT WAS PAID IN FULL WITH A CLEAR TITLE. THE PRICE WAS RIGHT AND THE PAYMENTS WERE A LOT LESS THAN I WAS PAYING FOR RENT EACH MONTH.

WE ONLY HAD A WEEK UNTIL WE HAD TO MOVE SO AFTER WORK WE BOUGHT OLD MATTRESSES AT THE THRIFT STORE FOR A FEW BUCKS EACH AND PULLED ALL THE COTTON OUT WHICH WE USED TO CHINK (FILL) THE CRACKS BETWEEN THE LOGS. WE HUNG A FRONT AND A BACK DOOR AND PUT VISQUEEN (PLASTIC) OVER THE HOLES WHERE WINDOWS BELONGED. WE BOUGHT AN OLD WOOD STOVE AND PUT IT IN THE AREA WE WOULD EVENTUALLY MAKE INTO A KITCHEN AND VENTED IT THROUGH THE CENTER OF THE WINDOW WHERE WE HAD PUT SHEET METAL IN THE HOLE FOR FIRE PROOFING. WE DECIDED ON THE AREA WE WOULD WANT FOR A BATHROOM AND PUT A WASH PAN ON A SMALL CABINET AND BOUGHT A HONEY BUCKET (A BIG POT TO USE AS THE TOILET) WHICH COULD BE DUMPED IN A HOLE OUTSIDE UNTIL WE ACTUALLY HAD A BATHROOM. BY APRIL FIRST WE HAD MOVED IN AND THE OLD LANDLORD COULD HAVE HIS PLACE BACK.

IT WAS STILL GETTING REALLY COLD IN APRIL SO I WOULD GET UP THREE OR FOUR TIMES A NIGHT TO ADD WOOD TO THE STOVE BUT WE WERE ALASKANS AND WE COULD DO IT. AFTER ALL, IN LATE MAY THE MELT OFF WOULD COME, THE ICE WOULD BREAK UP IN THE CHENA RIVER AND IT WOULD BE SPRING – GREAT, ONLY TWO MONTHS TILL SUMMER AND WE DIDN'T HAVE TO WASTE OUR MONEY PAYING RENT TO SOME JERK.

WE USED THE RENT MONEY WE HAD BEEN PAYING TO FIX UP OUR HOME. WE INSTALLED WINDOWS, INSULATION, PANNELING, CARPET, A KITCHEN, WALLS, A BATHROOM, A SEPTIC SYSTEM AND HAND DROVE A WELL IN THE BASEMENT, INSTALLED A WATER PRESSURE PUMP AND WE HAD ALL

THE COMFORTS OF HOME AND WE PAID CASH FOR THE MATERIAL EACH MONTH. BY THE TIME WE WERE DONE WE HAD A FOUR BEDROOM, TWO BATH LOG HOME LOCATED ON FIVE ACRES WHICH COULD BE DIVIDED ACCORDING TO THE CODE AND MORE HOUSES BUILT ON THOSE LOTS WHICH COULD BE USED AS RENTALS OR FOR SALE AND WE ONLY OWED $5,000.00 WHICH IS THE COST OF THE FIVE ACRES. DURING THIS CONSTRUCTION PHASE I HAD HELP FROM MY BROTHER TED AND SOME OF MY FRIENDS SEVERAL TIMES WHEN IT WAS REALLY NEEDED. THANK YOU! IN FACT FOR A TIME DURING ALL OF THIS MY BROTHER TED AND HIS FAMILY LIVED IN AN OLD CABIN HE AND I ASSEMBLED ON THE BACK OF THE FIVE ACRES OUT OF LOGS AND HE SHARED IN THE PAYMENTS ON THE PROPERTY. LATER, WHEN HE WANTED TO MOVE BACK TO TOWN, I BOUGHT HIS INTEREST BACK.

WITHIN FIVE YEARS WE HAD PAID IT ALL OFF. WE WERE HOMEOWNERS AND IT WAS MORTGAGE FREE! WE DIDN'T OWE A CENT ON IT! THERE WAS A LOT OF SATISFACTION IN WHAT WE HAD ACCOMPLISHED – PLUS WE HAD NOT WASTED OUR HARD EARNED MONEY ON RENT PAYMENTS. WE HAD A HOUSE THAT WAS PAID FOR. IT TAKES A LOT OF SELF DISCIPLINE TO DO WHAT WE DID AND YOU CAN'T WASTE YOUR MONEY ON A LOT OF UN-NECESSARY STUFF BUT WE DID IT AND YOU CAN DO IT, TOO! SURE, WE HAD SOME TOYS, WE HAD A DOG SLED AND SEVENTEEN DOGS SO WE COULD GO MUSHING IN THE FORESTS OF ALASKA, WE WENT CAMPING AND HUNTING, WE WENT OUT FOR DINNER SOMETIMES BUT WE DEDICATED OURSELVES (AFTER SELLING OUR TIME WORKING) TO FINISHING OUR HOME. HOW MANY PEOPLE CAN YOU NAME THAT WORK FOR A LIVING AND SUCCEED IN OWNING A HOME WITH NO MORTGAGE WITHIN FIVE YEARS? I CAN'T THINK OF MORE THAN A FEW THAT I KNOW BUT THEY WERE ALASKANS AND DIDN'T TRY TO KEEP UP WITH THE JONESES AS THE SAYING GOES. BESIDES THAT, EVERYONE THAT I KNEW RESPECTED WHAT WE WERE DOING AND WOULD COME FOR VISITS DURING THE CONSTRUCTION PHASE AND WOULD EVEN USE THE HONEY BUCKET AND DUMP IT.

IN A FEW MORE YEARS, AFTER I DIVIDED THE FIVE ACRES INTO LOTS, I BUILT A 2800 SQUARE FOOT HOUSE ON ONE LOT AND MOVED INTO IT AND SOLD THE LOG HOME TO A MILITARY FAMILY FOR A LOT MORE THAN WE HAD IN THE ENTIRE PROPERTY. EVENTUALLY WE MOVED TO ANOTHER ADVENTURE OUTSIDE ALASKA WITH MONEY IN OUR POCKET. BY THE WAY DID I MENTION THAT WHEN MY BROTHER AND I ARIVED IN ALASKA ON MY TWENTY-FOURTH BIRTHDAY THAT WE ONLY HAD $75.00 IN OUR POCKET? WE ONLY HAD $37.50 EACH AND OUR FAMILIES WERE STILL IN THE LOWER 48 SO WE GOT A JOB IMMEDIATELY AND WENT TO WORK ON BRINGING THEM TO ALASKA TO BE WITH US WHICH I SUCCEEDED IN DOING WITHIN A YEAR AND MY BROTHER IN TWO YEARS.

FOR SALE CHEAP

SOME PEOPLE MIGHT SAY TO ME, "YOU JUST LUCKED OUT WHEN YOU FOUND THAT DEAL!" THAT STATEMENT IS RIGHT AND IT IS WRONG! IT IS RIGHT BECAUSE MAYBE I WAS LUCKY (OR BLESSED) BUT IT IS ALSO WRONG BECAUSE WE WERE FORCED TO MOVE AND WERE WILLING TO SETTLE FOR A LOT LESS THAN WHAT WE REALLY WANTED AND I COULD SEE THE POTENTIAL THAT OLD LOG HOUSE HAD AND ESPECIALLY THE FIVE ACRES. THE ZONING IN THE NORTH STAR BOUROUGH FOR THAT AREA ALLOWED LOTS TO BE 1.25 ACRES SO I KNEW THAT I COULD DIVIDE IT AND DO A LOT MORE. I WAS 25 YEARS OLD – BY 30 I WAS A MILLIONAIRE!

YOU SHOULD LOOK FOR THAT OPPORTUNITY WHEN YOU ARE LOOKING FOR A HOUSE TO BUY. ONE THAT YOU CAN FIX UP AND MAKE IT INTO THE HOME OF YOUR DREAMS OR LATER RESELL OR RENT OUT.

THERE ARE MILLIONS OF RENTALS OUT THERE THAT THE OWNERS ARE TIRED OF HAVING TO PAINT AND FIX UP AFTER THE TENNANTS MOVE OUT. LOOK FOR PLACES WITH POTENTIAL! IF YOU SEE OLDER HOUSES IN AN AREA WHERE SOME NEW CONSTRUCTION IS UNDER WAY AND THE NEIGHBORHOOD IS OK, ESPECIALLY IF IT HAS ENOUGH PROPERTY TO DIVIDE, YOU MAY HAVE FOUND A GREAT DEAL. IT HAS TO BE SOMETHING YOU CAN AFFORD AND HAVE MONEY LEFT EACH MONTH FOR FIXING IT UP.

YOU CAN CHECK WITH ANY LOCAL TITLE COMPANY FOR INFORMATION ON ZONING, SUB-DIVIDING AND LEGAL PAPERWORK. REMEMBER THAT I SAID I BOUGHT THE OLD LOG HOUSE ON A CONTRACT OF SALE? SOMETIMES THAT IS OK BUT IT MUST BE LEGALLY DONE FOR YOUR OWN PROTECTION. I RECOMMEND THAT YOU USE A TITLE COMPANY WHO WILL RECORD THE DOCUMENTS AND INSURE THAT YOU HAVE A PROPER TITLE WHEN IT IS PAID OFF. YOU SHOULD ALSO USE A SURVEYOR FOR YOUR SURVEY AND RECORDABLE DIVISION OF THE LAND. ALL OF THIS IS NOT THAT EXPENSIVE AND IF YOU ARE BUYING A HOME THAT IS A LITTLE BELOW YOUR MEANS YOU CAN AFFORD TO DO IT CORRECTLY. I AM NOT A LAWYER EITHER AND IF YOU FEEL THAT YOU NEED LEGAL ADVICE MAYBE YOU SHOULD SPEND THE FEW DOLLARS IT WILL COST TO CONSULT WITH ONE SO THAT MISTAKES AREN'T MADE. THE TITLE COMPANY WILL SOMETIMES GIVE YOU ADVICE ALSO.

THERE ARE MANY MANY PLACES OUT THERE WHERE THE OWNER WILL SELL IT WITH A REASONABLE DOWN PAYMENT AND CARRY THE NOTE THEIRSELF, LETTING THOSE WITH IMPERFECT CREDIT BUY HOUSES. BUT BE CERTAIN TO SCRUTINIZE THE CONTRACT WITH A LAWYER IF NECESSARY AND USE A TITLE COMPANY TO INSURE IT IS ALL CORRECT.

BAD CREDIT? – YOU CAN STILL DO IT!

IF YOU HAVE BAD CREDIT THIS MAY BE THE OPPORTUNITY TO GET YOURSELF OUT OF THAT SITUATION BY SETTLING FOR LESS, PAYING OFF YOUR DEBTS, START THE FIX IT UP PROCESS AND IN A FEW YEARS OWN YOUR OWN HOME AND BECOME WEALTHY.

NOT ONLY ARE RENTAL LANDLORDS WANTING TO SELL THEIR RENTALS YOU MAY ALSO FIND REAL ESTATE AGENTS SELLING OWNER WILL CARRY (OWC) HOUSES AND LAND. SOME BANKS HAVE PROPERTY WHICH THEY HAVE FORECLOSED ON AND WANT TO SELL AND WILL FINANCE IT. THEY ARE IN THE MONEY BUSINESS – NOT THE REAL ESTATE BUSINESS. YOU SHOULD DRIVE AROUND AND LOOK FOR SALE SIGNS ON PROPERTY THAT THE OWNER WILL FINANCE IN AN AREA THAT HAS POTENTIAL. YOU CAN LOOK IN THE NEWSPAPERS AND THE FREE SHOPPER PAPERS IN YOUR AREA – THERE ARE PLENTY OF THEM AROUND SO START LOOKING AND USE PROFESSIONAL ASSISTANCE.

SELLER FINANCING WORKS WHEN IT IS DONE CORRECTLY AND IT IS A GREAT WAY TO FINANCE YOUR NEW HOME ESPECIALLY IF YOU HAVE NO CREDIT, BAD CREDIT OR A BANKRUPTCY OR MAYBE YOU HAVE AN INCOME WITH SOME CREDIT BUT CAN'T QUALIFY FOR A LOAN FOR SOME REASON. IF YOU FALL INTO THIS CATEGORY AND ARE THROWING AWAY YOUR HARD EARNED MONEY EVERY MONTH FOR RENT – QUIT! GO OUT AND FIND A HOME THAT THE OWNER WILL CARRY – AGAIN, SETTLE FOR LESS, PAY YOUR PAST DUE BILLS, RE-ESTABLISH GOOD CREDIT AND MAKE YOURSELF WEALTHY THE WORKING MAN AND WOMANS WAY!

EVEN IF YOU HAVE GOOD CREDIT YOU CAN USE WHAT YOU LEARN IN THIS BOOK AS A WAY TO GET AWAY FROM SURVIVAL – AND BROKE – TO BEING WEALTHY!

YOU CAN LIVE IN YOUR OWN HOME 10 YEARS – FREE!

I SAID, "YOU CAN LIVE IN YOUR OWN HOME 10 YEAR – FREE!" WELL, THEN I GUESS I HAVE TO SHOW YOU THAT YOU CAN.

I'M GOING TO USE SOME FIGURES IN THE FOLLOWING EXAMPLE FROM MY ORIGINAL WRITING OF THIS BOOK IN 1985. THERE MAY OR MAY NOT BE A HOUSE AVAILABLE IN THESE PRICE RANGES WHERE YOU ARE LOOKING BUT YOU CAN ADJUST THE FIGURES TO FIT YOUR SITUATION AND THE ECONOMY.

(1985) WE KNOW THAT YOU CAN'T GO OUT AND BUY A NEW HOME WITH THE NORMAL MORTGAGE AND AT THE PRICES FOR A HOME TODAY THAT FITS THE CATEGORY OF WHAT YOU REALLY WANT IN A HOME WITH PAYMENTS FOR 30 OR 40 YEARS, WHICH WOULD BE A HOUSE THAT YOU WILL LOSE IF YOU LOSE YOUR JOB. SO LET'S LOOK AT THE IDEA OF SETTLING FOR LESS AND BUYING AN OLDER HOME THAT HAS A LOT OF POTENTIAL AND HOPEFULLY WITH SOME LAND THAT IS BIG ENOUGH TO DIVIDE LATER ON.

THE POTENTIAL OF THE HOME IS WHATEVER YOU THINK IT CAN BE AFTER IT IS REMODELED AND ONE THAT WILL BE ATTRACTIVE AND COMFORTABLE FOR YOUR FAMILY.

LOOK AT IT WITH THE IDEA AND VISUALIZE WHAT IT WILL LOOK LIKE AFTER YOU HAVE MADE CHANGES TO IT SUCH AS REMOVING A NON-SUPPORTING WALL (CHECK WITH A FRIEND WHO KNOWS CONSTRUCTION) AND CHANGING THE KITCHEN, EXPANDING SOME ROOMS OR ADDING AN ADDITION (MORE ROOMS) ONTO THE HOUSE.

(1985). LET'S SAY YOU HAVE FOUND AN OLDER HOME THAT HAS A LOT OF POTENTIAL FOR $40,000.00. YOU CAN CHANGE THIS PRICE TO WHATEVER PRICE IS APPROPRIATE AND DO THE CALCULATIONS BELOW.

PROOF THAT YOU CAN LIVE THERE 10 YEARS FREE - FOLLOWS:

PURCHASE PRICE $40,000.00
MONTHLY PAYMENTS $450.31
TOTAL PAID IN ONE YEAR $5,403.72
TOTAL PAID IN TEN YEARS $54,037.20
TOTAL PAID TOWARD THE PRINCIPAL IN TEN YEARS $2,160.00
BALANCE OWED ON THE ORIGINAL LOAN AFTER 10 YEARS $37,840.00
INTEREST PAID IN TEN YEARS $51,877.20

SAVED ON INCOME TAXES IF YOU ARE IN THE 40% BRACKET $51,877.20 X 40% = $20,750.88

NOW LET'S ASSUME THE HOME APPRECIATED IN VALUE 4% A YEAR FOR TEN YEARS WHICH EQUALS 40% X $40,000.00 = $16,000.00 SO THE APPRECIATED VALUE OF THE HOME IS $56,000.00

SO WHAT DOES THIS MEAN?

IT LOOKS LIKE THIS:

IN TEN YEARS YOU PAID IN PAYMENTS $54,037.20
OUT OF THAT YOU PAID ON THE MORTGAGE $2,160.00
LOSS SO FAR $51,877.20
IN TEN YEARS YOU SAVED ON TAXES $20,750.88
LOSS SO FAR $31,126.32
IN TEN YEARS THE HOME APPRECIATED $16,000.00
LOSS ON YOUR INVESTMENT $15,126.32

NOW LET'S LOOK AT SOME MORE FIGURES:

IF YOU HAD BOUGHT THE $100,000.00 HOUSE YOUR PAYMENTS WOULD HAVE BEEN $1,125.78 PER MONTH, BUT YOU DIDN'T YOU BOUGHT THE $40,000.00 HOUSE WITH POTENTIAL AND YOUR PAYMENTS ARE ONLY $450.31 A MONTH. THIS IS A SAVINGS OF $675.47 PER MONTH.

NOW LET'S PUT $650.00 OF THE $675.47 SAVED PER MONTH INTO FIXING UP AND REMODELING THE HOUSE FOR ONLY 5 YEARS. THIS WILL TOTAL ONLY $39,000.00 INTO REMODELING. NOW LET'S SAY THAT EVERYTHING YOU DO INCREASES THE VALUE OF THE HOME BY 4% MORE THAN THE MONEY YOU ACTUALLY PUT INTO IT. NOTE: THE ACTUAL INCREASE IN VALUE MAY BE MORE OR LESS DEPENDING ON THE ECONOMY. ALSO, IT COULD BE A LOT MORE THAN 4% PROVIDED YOU DO MOST OR ALL OF THE WORK YOURSELVES. DO ALL OF IT IF YOU CAN! BUY BOOKS AT HOME DEPOT OR LOWES OR THE BOOK STORE ON HOW TO DO IT. USE FRIENDS OR FRIENDS OF FRIENDS OR FAMILYS HELP IF THEY ARE WILLING. USE CONTRACTORS ONLY IF YOU NEED TO. YOU CAN MAKE MONEY THAT YOU WOULD HAVE PAID THEM BY SAVING IT AND IF YOU USE CONTRACTORS SHOP FOR THE BEST PRICE AND PROFESSIONALISM. BUT FOR THIS CALCULATION LET'S USE 4%:

YOU INVESTED IN REMODELING $39,000.00
TIMES 4% APPRECIATION X TEN YEARS OR TIMES 40%
= $15,600.00

THE VALUE OF YOUR HOME AFTER TEN YEARS EQUALS:

APPRECIATED PURCHASE PRICE $56,000.00
REMODELING INVESTMENT $39,000.00
APPRECIATION ON REMODELING INVESTMENT $15,600.00
TOTAL APPRECIATED VALUE OF THE HOME $110,600.00

KEEP IN MIND THAT IF YOU DECIDED TO SELL YOUR HOME AT THIS TIME IT SHOULD BE WORTH $110,600.00. YOU ONLY OWE A BALANCE ON THE HOME OF $37,840.00 SO YOU COULD PUT $72,760.00 IN YOUR POCKET.

SO HOW DOES THIS LOOK PROFIT-WISE?

YOU PAID TOWARD THE PRINCIPAL $2,160.00
YOU OWE A BALANCE ON THE LOAN OF $37,840.00
YOU PAID IN INTEREST AFTER TAX CREDITS $31,126.32
YOU INVESTED IN REMODELING $39,000.00
YOUR TOTAL INVESTMENT IN THE HOME $110,126.32

IF THE VALUE OF THE HOME IS $110,600.00 LESS THE INVESTMENT IN THE HOME ABOVE WILL LEAVE A PROFIT OF $473.68

IF YOU SOLD THE HOME AND PAID OFF THE MORTGAGE YOU WILL ACTUALLY LIVE THERE FOR TEN YEAR FREE!

IF YOU KEEP IT YOU WILL BE LIVING AS GOOD AS THE JONESES AND PAYING A LOT LESS IN PAYMENTS.

A HUGE $40,000.00 BONUS………

WAIT A MINUTE! WE ONLY PUT $650.00 A MONTH INTO REMODELING FOR FIVE YEARS! WHAT DO I DO WITH THE EXTRA FIVES YEARS OF SAVING $675.00 A MONTH OUT OF THE TEN YEARS WE WERE TALKING ABOUT. THAT IS A $40,000.00 BONUS TO BUYING THE OLDER HOME AND FIXING IT UP. HAD YOU BOUGHT THE $100,000.00 HOME YOU WOULD BE MAKING PAYMENTS ON IT FOR ANOTHER 10 – 20 – OR 30 YEARS AT $1,125.78 A MONTH! HOWEVER, SINCE YOU BOUGHT THE OLDER HOME AND REMODELED WITH THAT EXTRA MONEY FOR FIVE YEARS YOU COULD, IF YOU LIKE, PAY THE EXTRA MONEY TOWARD THE MORTGAGE AND HAVE YOUR HOME ALMOST PAID OFF BY THE TIME THE TEN YEARS IS UP OR IT COULD GO INTO ANOTHER HOME JUST LIKE THE ONE YOU BOUGHT AND FIXED UP AND YOU CAN SELL IT OR RENT IT OUT.

THAT IS GREAT, ISN'T IT? YOU HAVE BOUGHT YOUR OWN HOME, REMODELED IT THE WAY YOU WANT IT AND IT'S PAID OFF IN TEN YEARS! IT'S WORTH OVER $100,000.00 AND YOU DIDN'T WASTE YOUR MONEY GIVING IT TO SOMEONE FOR RENT. YOU CAN LIVE THERE RENT AND PAYMENT FREE FOR THE REST OF YOUR LIFE IF YOU WANT TO.

IF YOU DECIDE TO SELL IT YOU CAN PUT A LOT OF MONEY IN YOUR POCKET TO BUY MORE PROPERTIES WITH. IF YOU BOUGHT LAND WITH YOUR OLDER HOME YOU CAN DIVIDE IT AND START ANOTHER HOME ON ONE OF THE EXTRA LOTS AND BECOME A LANDLORD WITH YOUR RENTALS RIGHT NEXT DOOR SO YOU CAN KEEP AN EYE ON THEM. THIS IS REAL WEALTH…..IF YOU PAY THE HOUSE OFF WITH THE EXTRA $40,000.00 YOU HAVE SAVED YOU WILL NOT LOSE YOUR HOME IF YOU SHOULD LOSE YOUR JOB. YOU HAVE DONE THIS IN TEN YEARS NOT THE TRADITIONAL LONG TERM LOANS OF 30 OR 40 YEARS ON NEW HOMES.

WHAT WOULD HAVE HAPPENED IF YOU HAD BOUGHT THE $100,000.00 NEW HOUSE INSTEAD? AT THIS FIXED RATE OF INTEREST WITH PAYMENTS OF $1,125.78 PER MONTH FOR 30 YEARS YOU WOULD END UP PAYING $405,280.80………………
WHAT?
$405,280.80 FOR A $100,000.00 HOME!

YOU SHOULD KEEP IN MIND THAT YOU DON'T HAVE TO SPEND $650.00 A MONTH ON REMODELING IF YOU DON'T WANT TO BUT THE OBJECT IS TO DO IT A RAPIDLY AS YOU CAN – GET ON THE ROAD TO WEALTH AS FAST AS YOU CAN. IT TAKES SELF DISCIPLINE! WE ALL HAVE A TENDENCY TO WANT THE TOYS IN LIFE AND TO GO INTO DEBT TO GET THEM SO DON'T MAKE THAT MISTAKE. SURE, YOU HAVE EXTRA MONEY FOR UNEXPECTED

THINGS THAT HAPPEN AND YOU WILL SPLURGE SOMETIME BUT GO RIGHT BACK TO THE PLAN AS FAST AS YOU CAN OR YOU WILL NOT SUCCEED, OK?

LET ME JUST SAY THIS. IF YOU CAN ONLY AFFORD TO PUT $325.00 A MONTH INTO REMODELING AND FIXING IT UP OR ONLY $100.00 A MONTH INTO YOUR OWN HOME THAT IS A LOT BETTER THAN RENTING AND WASTING YOUR HARD EARNED MONEY.

YOU CAN BUY LAND THAT IS BIG ENOUGH TO DIVIDE AND SPLIT IT INTO LOTS AND GET A MOBILE HOME FOR ONE OF THEM WHILE YOU ARE BUILDING A HOME ON ANOTHER LOT WITH THE MONEY YOU SAVE. IF YOU DO ALL THE WORK THAT YOU CAN YOU WILL HAVE A NICE HOME AND BECOME WEALTHY. IT MAY TAKE A LITTLE LONGER BUT YOU CAN DO IT AND YOU SHOULD.

SOME POINTERS ON THE CONTRACT

WHEN YOU BUY YOUR HOME, MOBILE HOME OR BARE LAND YOU SHOULD NEGOTIATE AS MANY OPTIONS WITH THE SELLER THAT ARE IN YOUR FAVOR AS YOU CAN GET.

SINCE YOU WILL BE TRYING TO FIND ONE WITH MORE LAND THAN YOU NEED THAT CAN BE DIVIDED YOU SHOULD GET THE SELLER TO AGREE THAT THEY WILL GIVE YOU PARTIAL RELEASE FOR THE LOT UPON RECEIPT OF PAYMENT EQUAL TO THE PRICE YOU ARE BUYING THE LAND FOR PER ACRE.

GET AN OPTION FOR EARLY PAYOFF WHICH WILL ALLOW YOU TO PAY OFF THE HOME ANY TIME WITHOUT A PRE-PAYMENT PENALTY AND ONE THAT ALLOWS YOU TO PAY EXTRA TOWARD THE PRINCIPAL BALANCE ANY TIME WITHOUT PENALTY.

NEGOTIATE THE BEST TERMS SUCH AS PRICE, DOWN PAYMENT AND INTEREST AS YOU CAN GET.

MAKE CERTAIN THE PROPERTY HAS LEGAL ACCESS AND UTILITIES.

MAKE CERTAIN THE PROPERTY DOESN'T HAVE ANY LEINS ON IT AND IS NOT ENCUMBERED OR MORTGAGED.

BE CERTAIN TO USE PROFESSIONALS FOR ASSISTANCE IN ALL OF THIS AND USE A TITLE COMPANY TO PROPERLY RECORD AND PROTECT YOUR INTERESTS.

LOOK IT OVER

WHEN YOU BUY BE CERTAIN TO LOOK IT OVER. LOOK FOR POWER, PHONES, WATER AND SEWER. LOOK UNDER THE HOUSE FOR ROT, TERMITES AND SETTLING; LOOK IN THE ATTIC FOR STAINS LEFT FROM ROOF LEAKS OR BROKEN TRUSSES AND INSULATION. LOOK AT EVERYTHING OR HAVE A HOME INSPECTION COMPANY GIVE YOU A REPORT ON THE CONDITION OF THE HOME. IT'S ISN'T THAT YOU WILL NOT BUY THE HOME IF IT HAS PROBLEMS BUT THAT YOU WANT TO BE FULLY INFORMED SO THAT YOU WILL BE ABLE TO DETERMINE THE COST INVOLVED AND THE TIME NEEDED TO COMPLETE THE REPAIRS. YOU CAN GET ESTIMATES FROM CONTRACTORS, IF YOU LIKE AND USE THEM TO NEGOTIATE WITH THE SELLER EVEN THOUGH YOU MAY BE DOING MOST OF THE WORK YOURSELF. THE MORE YOU KNOW ABOUT THE HOUSE AND THE LAND THE BETTER YOU CAN NEGOTIATE ITEMS THAT WILL BE IN YOUR FAVOR AND SAVE YOU MONEY.

BE CERTAIN TO CHECK THE RULES FOR DIVIDING LAND IN THE AREA WITH THE COUNTY BUILDING AND SAFETY OR SOME SUCH DEPARTMENT. MAKE CERTAIN THE LAND IS DIVISABLE AND DOESN'T HAVE HUGE CREEK BOTTOMS OR WET ZONES AND MORE THAT WILL IMPAIR DIVIDING IT OR STOP YOUR HOME CONSTRUCTION. IF YOU DON'T KNOW ANYTHING ABOUT BUYING YOU CAN SPEND SOME TIME LEARNING BY LOOKING AT PLACES WITH A REAL ESTATE AGENT AND GATHER POINTERS THAT YOU CAN USE LATER. YOU CAN EVEN USE THE REAL ESTATE AGENT TO ACTUALLY HELP FINALIZE THE DEAL BY PAYING THEM A SMALL COMMISSION EVEN IF IT IS LAND THAT THEY DON'T HAVE LISTED OR EVEN IF IT IS FOR SALE BY THE OWNER. TALK TO ONE AND SEE WHAT THEY SAY.

NOT ONLY WILL YOU BE LOOKING AT THE HOME AND LAND ITSELF BUT YOU SHOULD BE LOOKING AROUND THE AREA IN GENERAL. IS IT DETERIORATING OR IS IT GROWING WITH SOME NEW PLACES GOING IN?

THEN LOOK AT THE BIGGER SCENE. IS THE LAND LOCATED IN THE PATH OF PROGRESS FOR THE CLOSEST CITY OR TOWN? COULD THE ROAD YOUR HOME WILL BE ON BECOME A MAIN HIGHWAY OR FREEWAY SOMEDAY? COULD IT BECOME A COMMERCIAL AREA IN A FEW YEARS?

LOOK AT THE IMMEDIATE VALUE TO YOU AS A HOME THAT YOU CAN AFFORD AND ONE THAT YOU CAN AFFORD TO FIX UP AND/OR DIVIDE THE LAND AND SELL LOTS OR BUILD ON! LOOK AT THE FUTURE POSSIBILITIES THAT MAY COST YOU MONEY OR MAY MAKE YOU WEALTHY!

RENTERS DON'T HAVE TO BE RENTERS

JUST REMEMBER, IF YOU'RE A RENTER – YOU DON'T HAVE TO BE! I'VE SEEN THE AMOUNT OF MONEY THAT IT TAKES TO MOVE INTO AN APARTMENT OR TO RENT A HOUSE AND BELIEVE ME THERE ARE HOMES OUT THERE THAT YOU CAN BUY FOR A DOWN PAYMENT OF ABOUT WHAT YOU HAVE TO SHELL OUT JUST TO GET SITUATED IN A RENTAL. LOOK IN THE LOCAL NEWSPAPERS, LOOK IN FREE SHOPPERS GUIDES, DRIVE AROUND AND LOOK FOR HOMES WITH A FOR-SALE SIGN. EVEN REALTORS WILL LIST AND SELL HOMES THAT CAN BE OWNER FINANCED WITH LOW DOWN PAYMENTS. IN ADDITION, YOU CAN ALWAYS MAKE AN OFFER ON A HOME THEY HAVE LISTED TO SEE WHAT THE SELLER WILL TAKE. JUST BECAUSE THEY HAVE TERMS THAT THEY ARE ASKING FOR DOESN'T MEAN THEY WILL NOT CONSIDER OR TAKE AN OFFER.

REAL ESTATE AGENTS MAKE THEIR LIVING BY SELLING HOMES OR LAND ON A COMMISSION BASIS. ANY AGENT CAN SELL ANY OTHER AGENTS HOME OR LAND AND WILL NEGOTIATE A COMMISSION WITH THE OTHER AGENT. FIND ONE THAT WILL WORK WITH AND FOR YOU THAT YOU ARE COMFORTABLE WITH AND TRUST. THEY WILL EVEN HELP YOU BUY A HOUSE OR LAND THAT IS NOT LISTED WITH ANYONE. THEY WORK FOR YOU AND YOU PAY THEM TO DO THE PAPERWORK. BE CERTAIN TO NEGOTIATE A FEE WITH THEM THAT IS IN YOUR BEST INTEREST.

EVEN IF YOU HAVE SHAKEY CREDIT THE SELLER CAN'T LOSE. IF YOU DEFAULT ON YOUR PAYMENTS THEY SIMPLY GET THE HOUSE BACK SO OWNER/SELLERS WILL DO THIS MOST OF THE TIME – JUST USE A TITLE COMPANY AFTER YOU HAVE NEGOTIATED THE BEST TERMS THAT YOU CAN GET. I SELL HOMES OR LAND THAT I OWN WHENEVER I CAN. WITH INTEREST, I USUALLY MAKE DOUBLE AND SOMETIMES TRIPPLE THE PRICE THAT I SOLD IT FOR BY THE END OF THE MORTGAGE AND I CAN ALWAYS SELL THE NOTE TO MORTGAGE BUYERS FOR CASH ANY TIME I WANT – AT A DISCOUNT.

EVEN IF YOU HAVE BAD CREDIT YOU CAN FIND SOMEONE LIKE ME WHO WILL SELL YOU A HOME OR LAND. SO DO THAT! DON'T WASTE YOUR MONEY ON RENT! REBUILD YOUR CREDIT BY LIVING SLIGHTLY BELOW YOUR MEANS AND GET ON THE ROAD TO WEALTH THE WORKING MAN AND WOMANS WAY!

DON'T BE A HOME BUYER/LOSER

IF YOU ARE A HOME BUYER/LOSER YOU DON'T HAVE TO BE! STUDY THE INFORMATION YOU NOW HAVE, DECIDE WHICH APPROACH SUITS YOU AND THEN GO OUT AND PUT TOGETHER A HOME DEAL FOR YOURSELF THAT YOU CAN REALLY AFFORD WHICH WILL LET YOU END UP LIVING THERE FOR YEARS – FREE, AS WE FIGURED OUT EARLIER IN THIS BOOK.

IF YOU HAVE ALREADY BOUGHT ONE OF THOSE BIG HOMES WITH A LONG MORTGAGE AND HIGH INTEREST YOU CAN STILL USE THIS APPROACH TO WEALTH. IF YOU DON'T HAVE ANY MONEY LEFT AFTER PAYING YOUR BILLS AND PAYMENTS EVERY MONTH THEN YOU SHOULD THINK ABOUT POSSIBLY SELLING AND SETTLING FOR SOMETHING LESS – JUST FOR A LITTLE WHILE. THINK ABOUT WHAT COULD HAPPEN IF YOU LOST YOUR JOB – WOULD YOU SOON LOSE YOUR CAR? THEN LOSE YOUR HOME? ARE YOU PUTTING ANY MONEY IN THE BANK TO COVER THAT POSSIBILITY?

IF YOU STILL HAVE MONEY LEFT OVER EVERY MONTH AND CAN AFFORD TO KEEP THAT BIG, NEW HOME AND AT THE SAME TIME PURCHASE ONE OF THE OLDER HOMES OR LAND AS WE ARE DISCUSSING THEN YOU SHOULD DO THAT. SLOW DOWN ON THE WASTED MONEY AND CUT BACK OR WAIT ON THE TOYS AND LOOK AROUND FOR A HOME THAT COULD MAKE YOU WEALTHY. BUY IT, REMODEL AND FIX IT OR EXPAND IT AND MAKE IT INTO A VERY VALUABLE PIECE OF PROPERTY. YOU CAN BECOME WEALTHY!

REMODEL IT – EXPAND IT – CHANGE IT – REDESIGN IT

IF YOU ALREADY OWN AN OLDER HOME AND ARE CONSIDERING SELLING IT, MAYBE YOU SHOULD TAKE ANOTHER LOOK AT IT TO SEE IF REMODELING IT OR EXPANDING IT WILL INCREASE ITS VALUE, OR, WILL YOU END UP WITH SOMETHING THAT YOU REALLY LIKE AND WOULD BE HAPPY TO LIVE IN? MAYBE YOU SHOULD LOOK AT THE ACTUAL LONG TERM COST OF A NEW HOME BEFORE YOU BUY ONE, SELL OUT AND MOVE. IF YOU CAN FIX UP THE ONE YOU NOW HAVE AND IF YOU WILL BE HAPPY WITH IT AFTERWARDS, YOU PROBABLY WILL BE A LOT BETTER OFF FINANCIALLY. YOU CAN DO THE REMODELING AS YOU CAN AFFORD IT ….. $100.00 THIS MONTH ….. $300.00 THE NEXT MONTH ….. ETC!

IF YOU ARE LOOKING AT AN OLDER HOME TAKE A TAPE MEASURE AND SOME PAPER AND A PEN OR PENCIL WITH YOU AND TAKE ALL THE MEASUREMENTS AND MAKE A SKETCH OF THE HOME WHILE YOU ARE STANDING IN IT. AFTER YOU GET HOME PUT IT ON SOME DRAFTING PAPER AND SEE WHAT CHANGES COULD BE MADE THAT WOULD MAKE THE HOME MORE LIVABLE. USE MORE PAPER AND DO THIS SEVERAL TIMES WITH YOUR SPOUSE AND LOOK AT ALL OF THE POSSIBILITIES. YOU COULD EVEN TAKE YOUR SKETCHES TO A DRAFTSMAN AND ASK FOR AN OPINION. THEY ARE REASONABLE AND WILL EVEN DRAW PROFESSIONAL PLANS FOR YOU AT A REASONABLE COST WHICH COULD BE USED AT THE COUNTY OR CITY LEVEL FOR YOUR PERMITS. YOU CAN TAKE YOUR PLANS TO A BUILDING SUPPLY STORE AND GET PRICES FOR THE MATERIAL NEEDED TO MAKE THE CHANGES. WITH PLANS YOU WILL ALSO BE ABLE TO GET QUOTES FROM CONTRACTORS TO DO THE PORTION OF THE WORK THAT YOU CAN'T DO. WATCH THEM OR BETTER YET, WORK WITH THEM FOR A DISCOUNT OFF OF THEIR QUOTE, WHILE THEY ARE DOING IT AND MAYBE YOU CAN DO THAT PART THE NEXT TIME YOURSELF.

THERE IS A LOT OF MONEY TO BE MADE ON THESE OLDER HOMES. SOMETIMES A SMALL INVESTMENT WILL RETURN FOUR OR FIVE TIMES THE AMOUNT YOU INVEST! I HOPE THAT AFTER READING THIS BOOK YOU WILL HAVE GAINED ENOUGH INFORMATION TO GO OUT AND BUY YOUR HOME. SOMETIMES SELLERS WILL TAKE SOMETHING IN TRADE LIKE A CAR, PICK UP OR MOTORHOME. I HAVE! THE GUY HAD A MOTORHOME THAT I REALLY LIKED SO I TOOK IT AS A DOWN PAYMENT.

DO IT! BECOME WEALTHY THE WORKING MAN AND WOMANS WAY TO WEALTH!

I HAVE INSERTED A FEW DRAWINGS OF OLDER HOMES AS EXAMPLES OF WHAT CAN BE DONE TO MAKE THEM MORE MODERN. OF COURSE, THERE ARE A NUMBER OF DIFFERENT WAYS TO REMODEL THEM – CAN YOU SEE ANY?

SOME OLDER HOMES ARE BUILT ON LARGE LOTS AND OTHER LOTS ARE VERY SMALL SO IF YOU INTEND TO EXPAND THE HOME YOU SHOULD MAKE CERTAIN THAT THE LOT IS BIG ENOUGH TO MEET THE ZONING REQUIREMENTS.

LOOK OVER THE SKETCHES. THEY ARE REALLY SIMPLE AND JUST SKETCHES AND MEASUREMENTS THAT I TOOK OF OLDER HOMES. LATER I WOULD SIT DOWN WITH DRAFTING PAPER AND MAKE THEM MORE DETAILED AND TO SCALE. TRY IT YOURSELF.

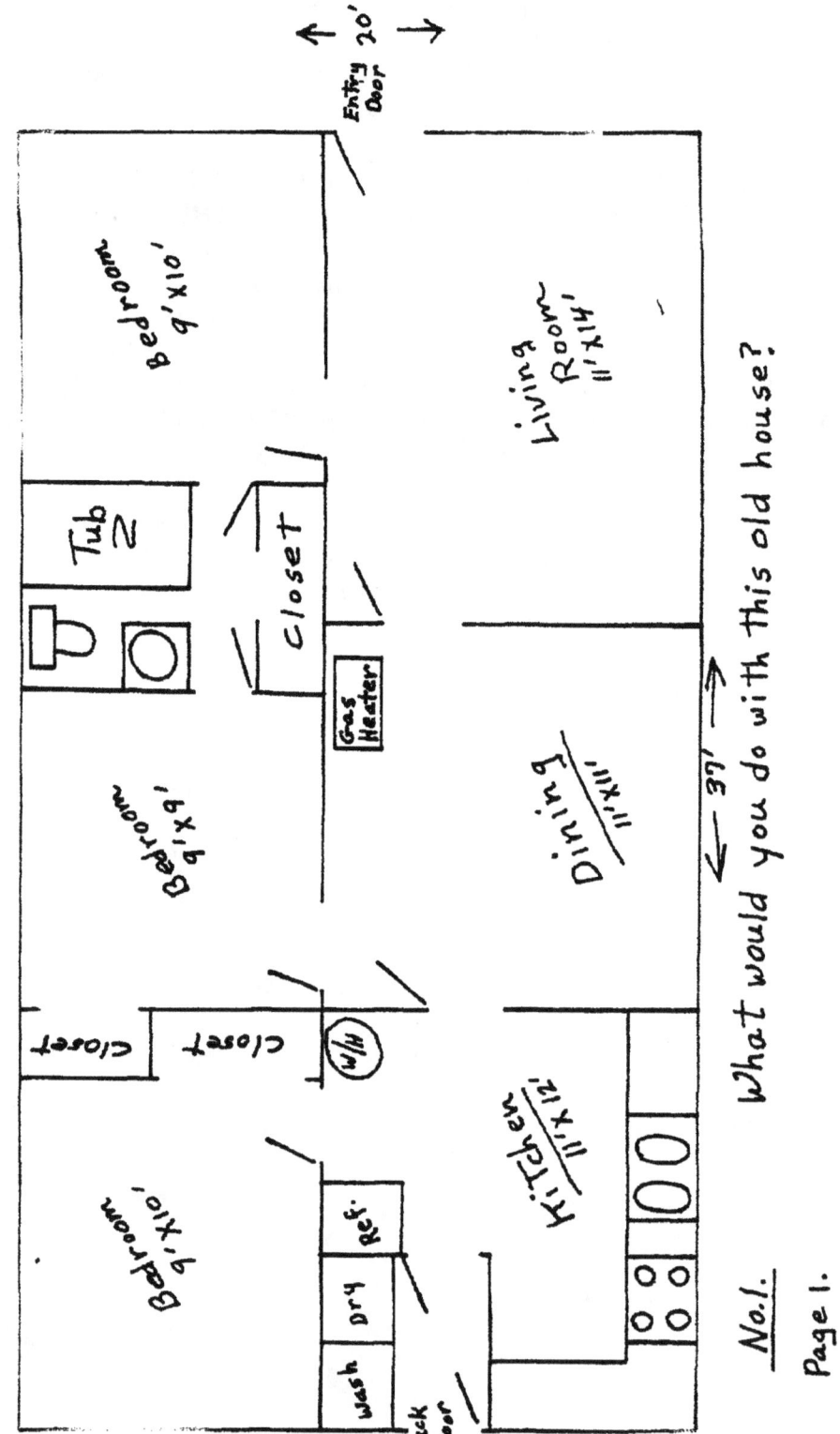

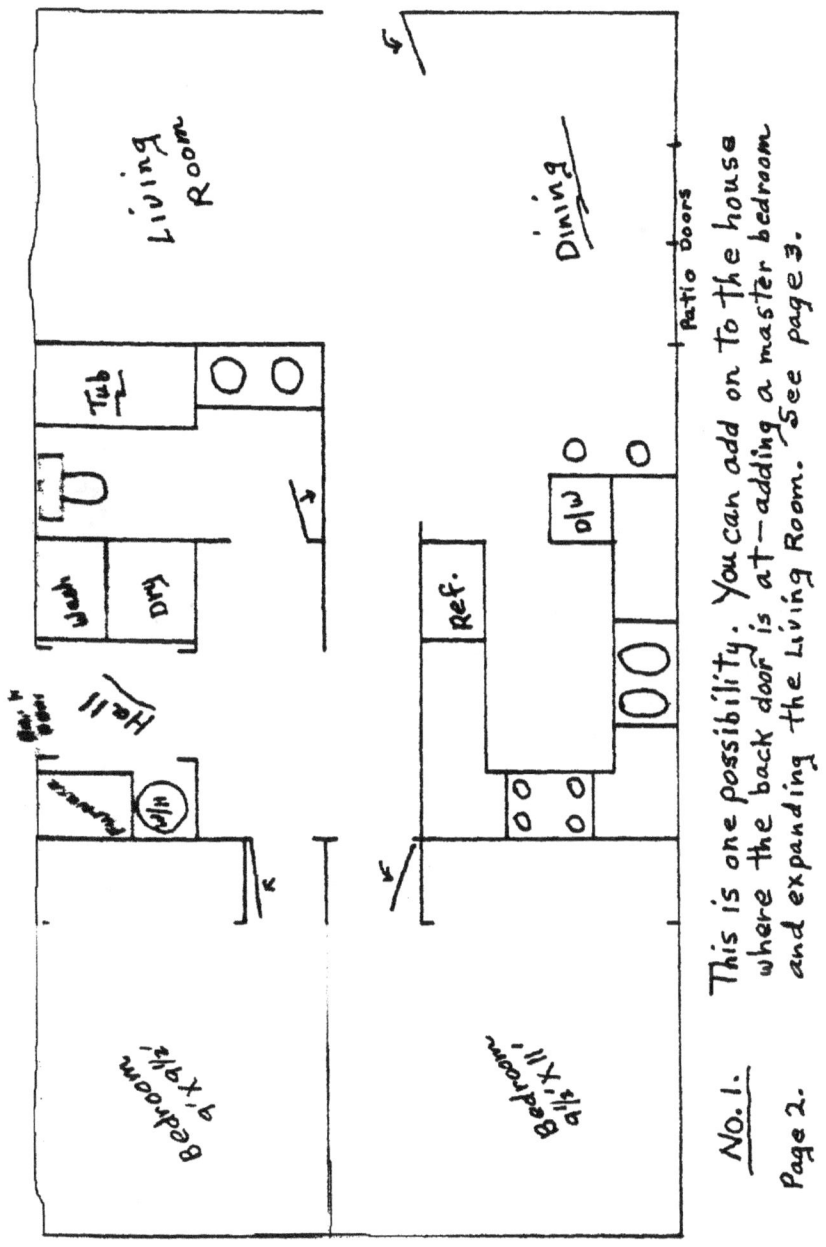

No. 1.

This is one possibility. You can add on to the house where the back door is at—adding a master bedroom and expanding the Living Room. See page 3.

Page 2.

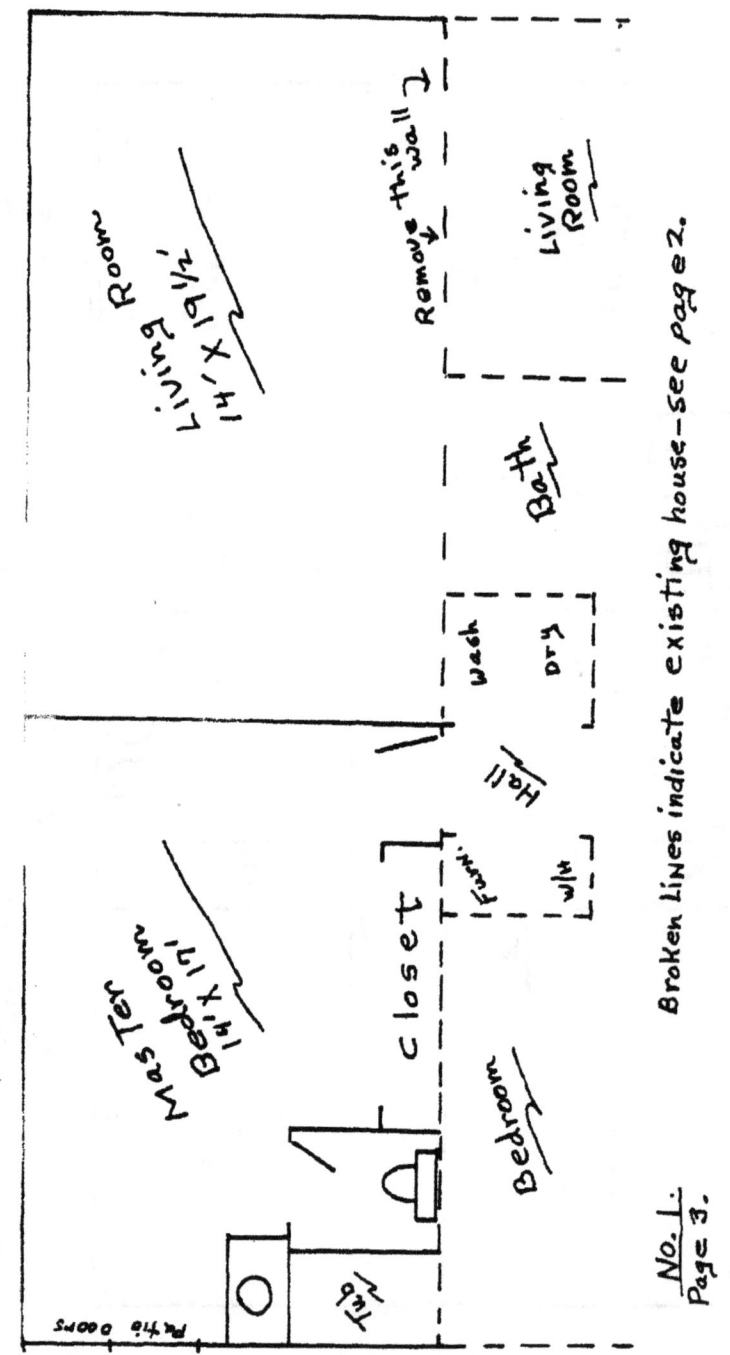

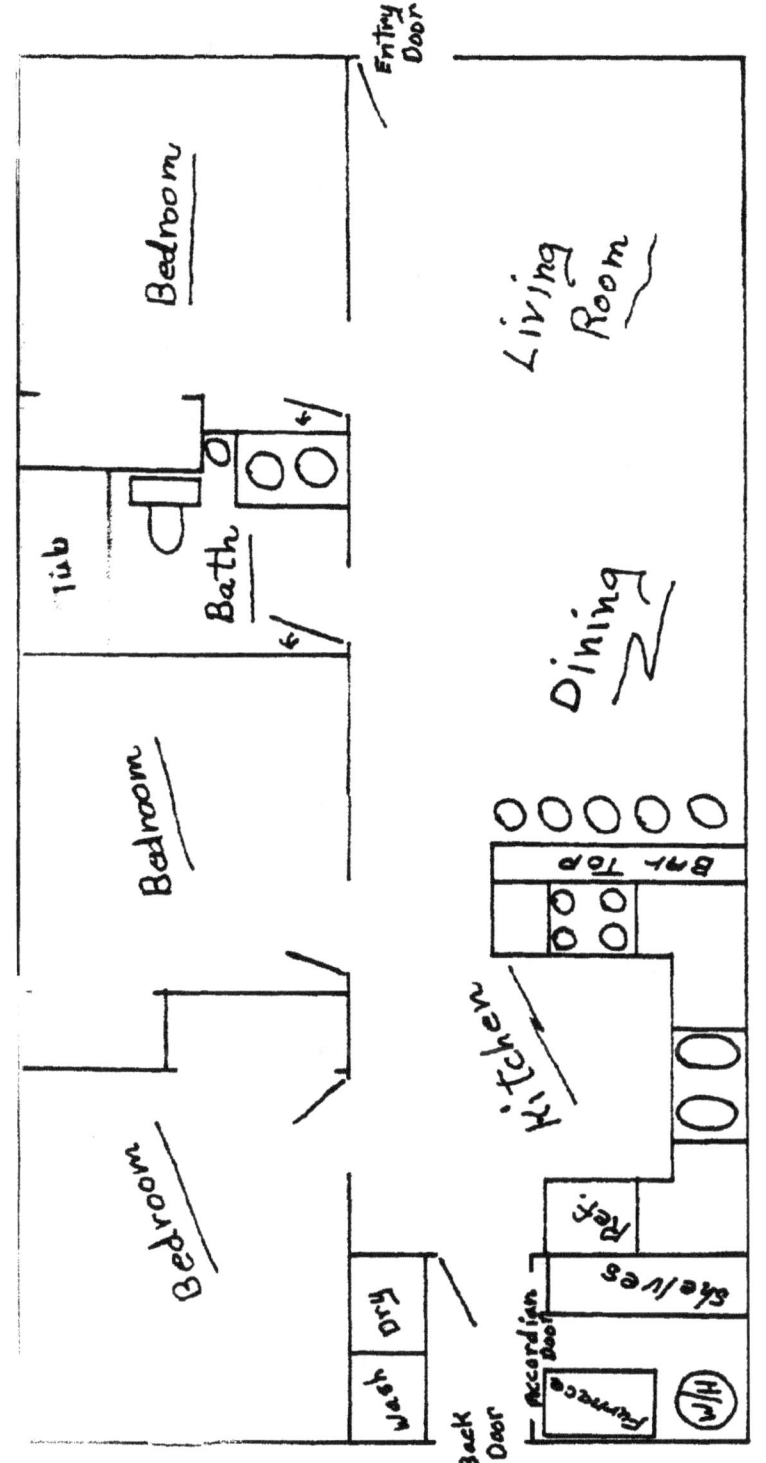

No. 1. Option 1. Use this plan if the land is too small to expand on.

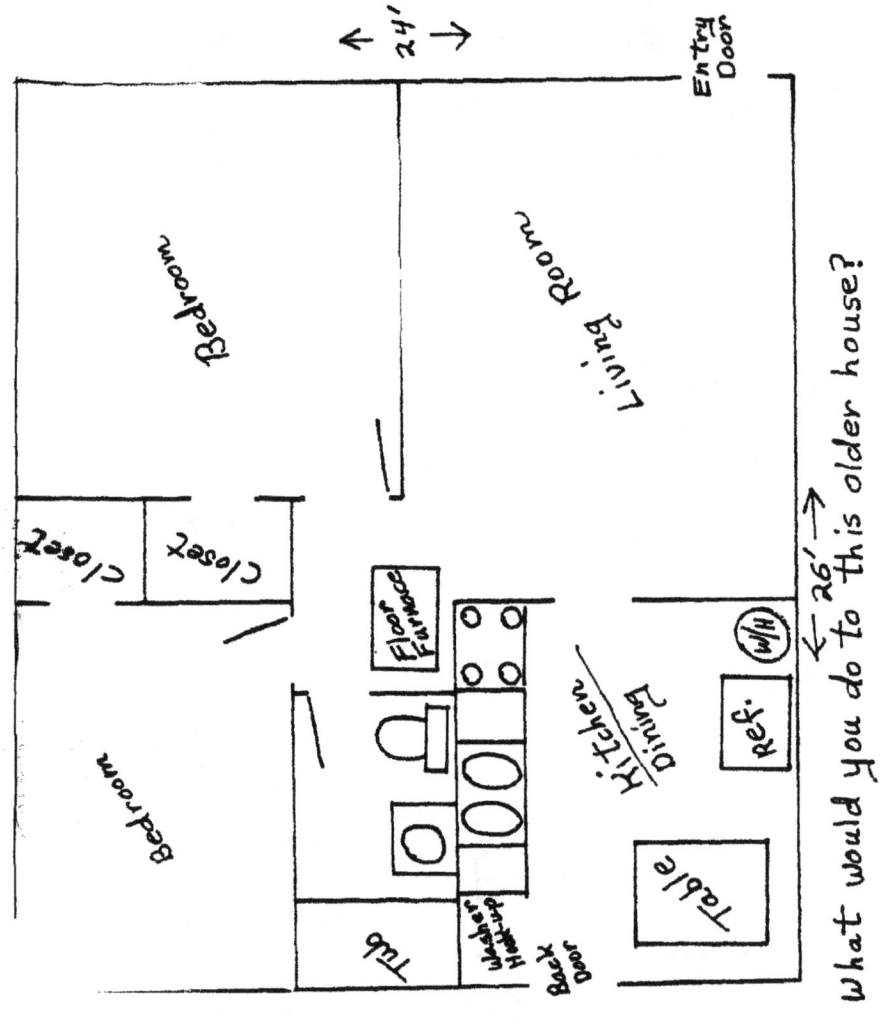

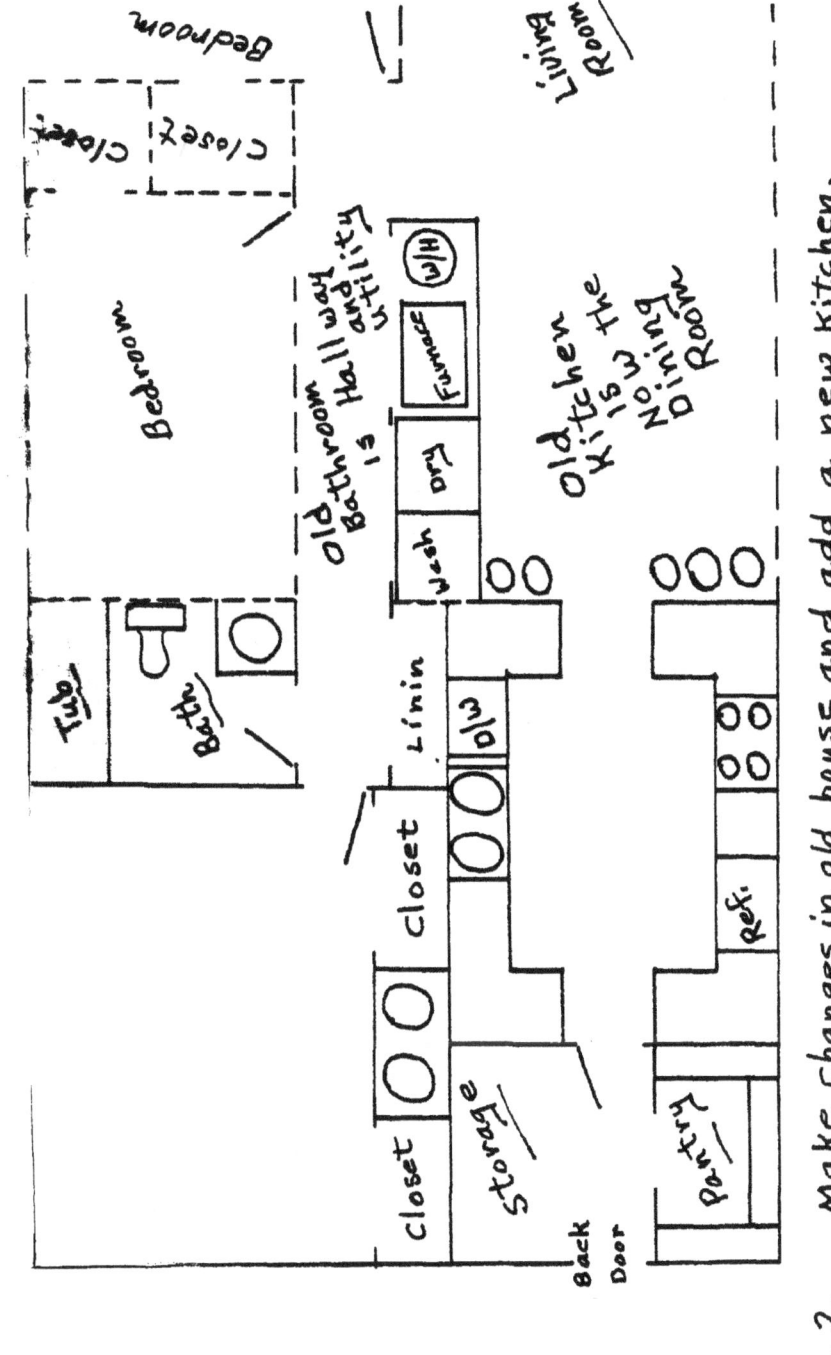

No. 2, Page 2.

Make changes in old house and add a new kitchen, pantry, storage, bathroom and Master Bedroom. Broken Lines indicate existing house. See page 1.

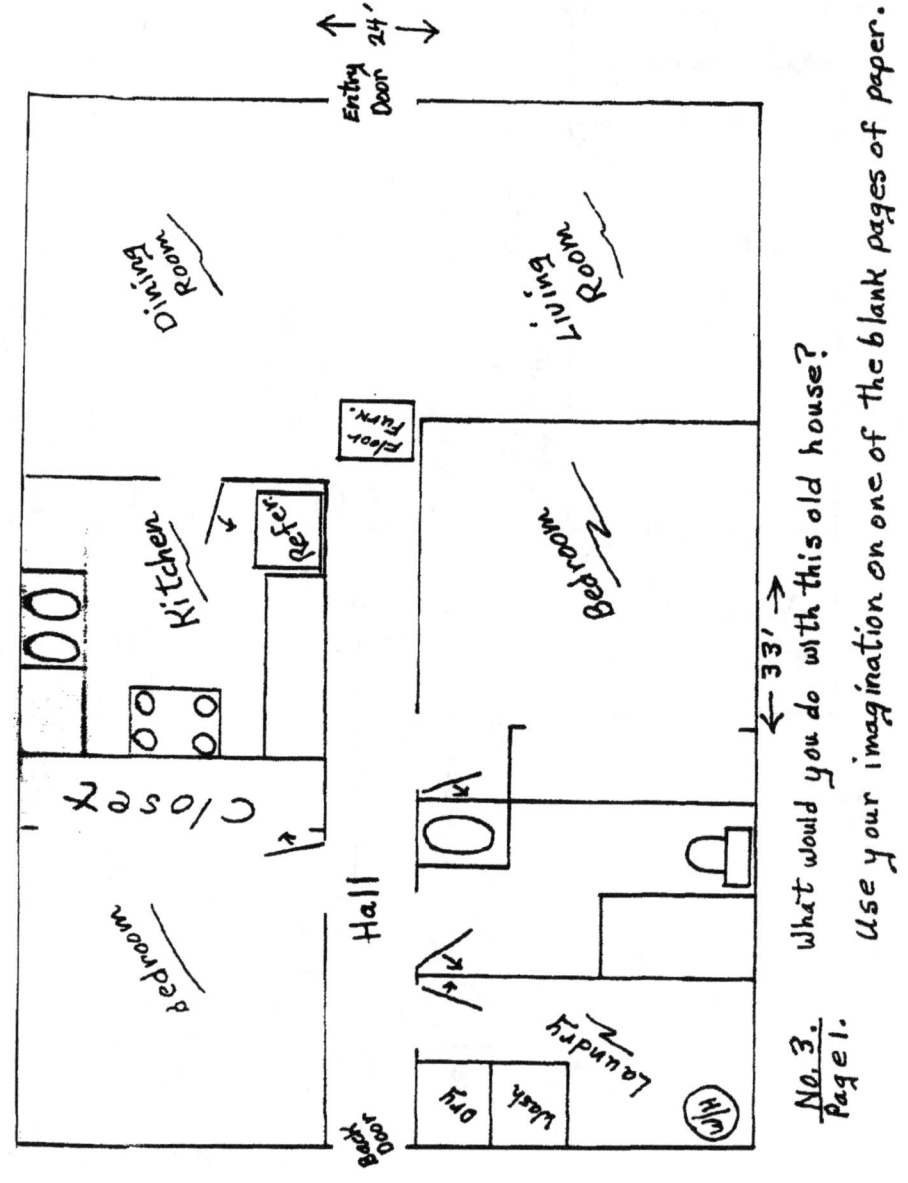

No. 4.
Page 1.

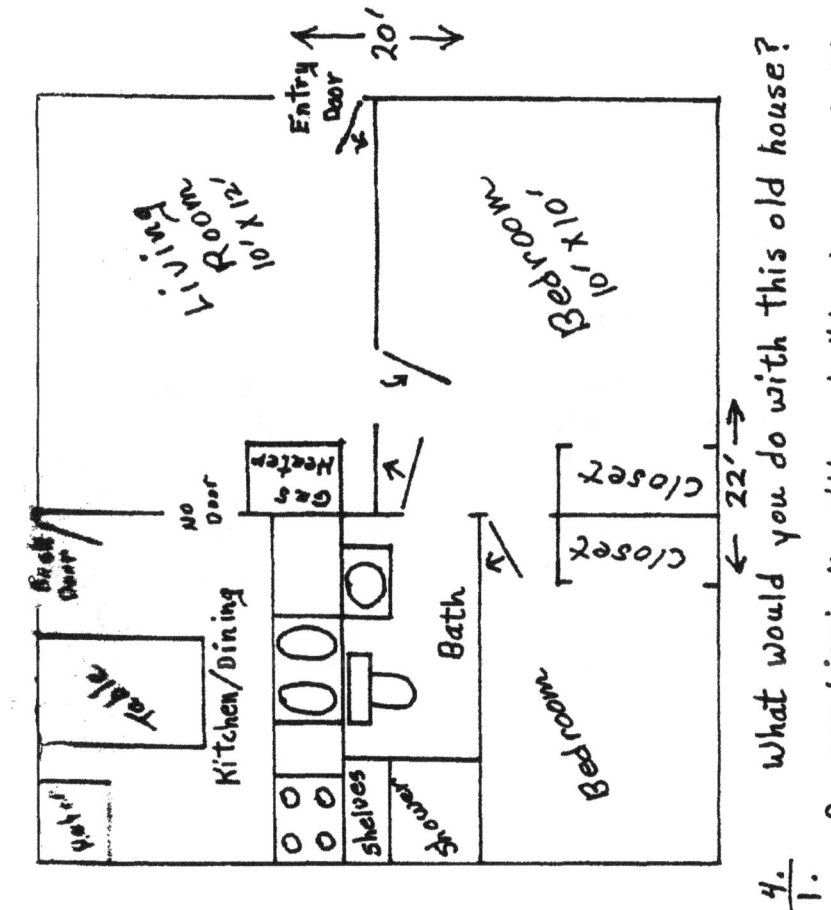

What would you do with this old house?

Answer: Live in it until you build a house onto it, then make this into a garage...... This is the house my Dad and brother built when I was a Kid. They intended to use it as the garage once the house was built onto it.

WE'RE GOING TO UPSET A FEW PEOPLE!

THE RICH PEOPLE THAT WANT TO LOAN YOU HUNDREDS OF THOUSANDS OF DOLLARS TO BUY A NEW HOME, A LOT OF NEW HOME DEVELOPERS, SOME REAL ESTATE AGENCIES AND MORTGAGE COMPANIES WILL BE MAD AT ME FOR WHAT I HAVE SHOWN YOU BECAUSE THEY MAKE THEIR FORTUNES OFF OF THE SALE OF NEW HOMES WITH LONG TERM MORTGAGES BUT I DON'T CARE. I WROTE THIS BOOK TO SHOW YOU HOW TO BECOME WEALTHY WITH YOUR MONEY – THE MONEY YOU NOW THROW AWAY EVERY MONTH.

ANOTHER OPTIONAL APPROACH

THERE WILL BE TIMES WHEN YOU JUST CAN'T FIND AN OLDER HOME WITH POTENTIAL IN A SUITABLE AREA OR AT THE RIGHT PRICE OR MAYBE YOUR EXPECTATIONS A TOO HIGH. MAYBE THE HOUSE YOU ARE LOOKING AT ISN'T AS UN-INHABITABLE AS YOU THINK IT IS. DO YOU REMEMBER THE 1903 HOUSE THAT I BOUGHT IN FAIRBANKS ALASKA?

PERHAPS THE OLDER HOME IDEA IS JUST NOT SUITABLE FOR YOU OR YOUR FAMILY.

IF THAT IS THE CASE THE NEXT APPROACH MAY WORK FOR YOU AND STILL LET YOU GET WEALTHY. IF I LOST MY JOB WHICH WOULD CAUSE ME TO LOSE MY HOME THEN I AM BROKE AS FAR AS I AM CONCERNED BUT IF MY HOME WAS SECURE EVEN IF I LOST MY JOB FOR FIVE YEARS THEN I AM WEALTHY! THIS OPTION IS A GOOD ONE UNDER SOME CIRCUMSTANCES EVEN THOUGH IT MAY TAKE A LITTLE LONGER TO BECOME A REALITY. I CALL IT SETTLING FOR LESS.

WE MUST SETTLE FOR LESS

EARLIER I SAID THAT A FEW DECADES AGO PEOPLE IN AMERICAN WERE MOSTLY POOR PEOPLE AND THAT BEING POOR WAS GENERALLY ACCEPTED. THERE WERE ACTUALLY FAMILIES WHERE ONE OF THEM AT LEAST WOULD STARVE TO DEATH OR THAT WOULD HAVE TO LIVE UNDER BRIDGES OR IN CAMPS THAT WERE FULL OF POOR FAMILIES.

WHEN I WAS YOUNG I CAN REMEMBER MY MOTHER AND FATHER TAKING FOOD TO FAMILIES DOWN THE ROAD WHO WERE REALLY HAVING A HARD TIME.

WITH THE ECONOMY THE WAY IT IS TODAY I BELIEVE THAT WE REALLY CAN'T AFFORD TO LOOK WEALTHY WHEN WE'RE NOT. PEOPLE ARE STARTING TO REALIZE AND ACCEPT THE FACT THAT WE MUST ALL SAVE ON UTILITIES, AUTOMOBILE GAS AND OUR HOME COSTS. WE MUST TIGHTEN OUR BELTS A LITTLE. WE MUST SETTLE FOR LESS. WE MUST LIVE WITHIN OUR MEANS.

WE ALL WANT TO LIVE IN A MANSION BUT REALLY, WHO CAN AFFORD THE HUGE COST AND UPKEEP AND TAXES? THOSE MANSIONS ARE ON THE WAY OUT AND MOST ALL OF US AND THE DEVELOPERS KNOW THAT SO THE BUILDERS ARE BUILDING STARTER HOMES IN THE 1,200 SQUARE FOOT RANGE OR SMALLER SO THAT PEOPLE CAN AFFORD TO BUY THEM. THAT IS THE PROBLEM WITH THOSE B R O K E PEOPLE – THEY BUY A BIG HOME THAT THEY REALLY WANT BUT THEN FIND THAT IT REALLY STRETCHES THEIR BUDGET TO PAY THE PAYMENTS AND WHEN HARD TIMES COME THEY END UP LOSING IT. WHAT DO THEY DO AFTER THAT AND WHERE DO THEY GO? THEY'VE GOT A BIG PROBLEM – ONE THAT YOU ARE TRYING TO ELIMINATE!

THERE IS A WAY TO BECOME WEALTHY AND IT IS CALLED SETTLING FOR LESS.

BUY ONE OF THOSE STARTER HOMES THAT MAY BE ONE HALF THE SQUARE FOOTAGE THAT YOU WANT BUT DON'T BUY ONE IN THOSE NEW HOUSING DEVELOPMENTS. BUY ONE THAT YOU CAN ADD ON SOME ROOMS AND TURN IT INTO THE HOME OF YOUR DREAMS.

WE WILL DISCUSS THIS IDEA MORE IN THE NEXT CHAPTER.

BUT – I WANT A BIG ONE

THE QUESTION HERE IS "HOW CAN I GET A HOME AT A PRICE I CAN AFFORD WHEN I WANT A BIG ONE?"

BACK IN THE PIONEER DAYS YOU JUST WENT OUT, CUT SOME DOWN SOME TREES, PUT UP THE WALLS AND A ROOF WITH SOD AND STRAW TO SHED THE WATER AND YOU HAD A MODERN HOME LIKE EVERYONE ELSE. IN THE DAYS WHEN MOST OF US WERE POOR WE WORKED FOR SOMEONE IN EXCHANGE FOR AN OLD SHACK TO LIVE IN OR WE LIVED IN CARDBOARD BOXES OR SHEDS OR WHATEVER COVER WE COULD FIND. LOOK AT WHAT THE MEDIA CALLS "THE THIRD WORLD COUNTRIES", MANY OF THOSE POOR PEOPLE STILL LIVE THAT WAY OR EVEN WORSE.

WHEN TIMES ARE GOOD IN AMERICA AND WE ARE PROSPERING WE SIMPLY GO OUT AND BUY A NEW HOME AT WHATEVER THE GOING PRICE IS THAT WE LIKE, WHICH MAY BE A MISTAKE. IF YOU REALLY LOOK AT OUR ECONOMY TODAY YOU WILL FIND THAT WE MUST STOP THROWING AWAY OUR HARD EARNED MONEY, THAT IS, IF WE WANT ANYTHING LEFT AFTER A LIFETIME OF WORK! WE DON'T MIND WORKING! IT'S JUST THAT WE WANT SOMETHING LEFT FOR OURSELVES TO ENJOY WHILE WE ARE YOUNG ENOUGH TO ENJOY IT. WE WANT TO SEE THAT WE HAVE ACCOMPLISHED SOMETHING IN OUR LIFE AND WE WANT THE OPPORTUNITY TO BECOME WEALTHY. WE WOULD LIKE TO LIVE EACH DAY IN COMFORT WITH SOME WORLDLY PLEASURES AND TOYS TO PLAY WITH. SO HOW CAN WE DO IT?

WE ALREADY KNOW THAT WE CAN'T GO OUT AND BUY A BIG NEW HOME WITH A LONG TERM MORTGAGE WHICH STRETCHES OUR BUDGET TO IT'S LIMIT BECAUSE WE WILL END UP BROKE IF SOMETHING GOES WRONG.

WE DO KNOW THAT WE CAN LOOK FOR AN OLDER HOME PREFERRABLY WITH EXTRA LAND THAT CAN BE DIVIDED. WE KNOW THAT WE CAN BUY AN OLDER HOME EVEN IF IT DOESN'T HAVE EXTRA LAND IF WE CAN'T FIND THE PERFECT ONE. WE KNOW THAT WE CAN JUST BUY BARE LAND BIG ENOUGH TO DIVIDE AND PUT A MOBILE HOME ON ONE OF THE LOTS WHILE WE ARE BUILDING A HOME ON ANOTHER ONE. WE KNOW THAT WE SHOULD LOOK FOR ONE IN THE PATH OF GROWTH AND IF POSSIBLE ON A ROAD AND IN AN AREA THAT HAS POTENTIAL.

IN SOME TOWNS WE COULD BUY AN OLDER BUILDING THAT WAS USED COMMERCIALLY AND SPLIT PART OF IT INTO LIVING QUARTERS FOR A RESIDENCE AND LATER USE PART OF IT FOR A STORE OF SOME SORT.

MANY YEARS AGO SOME PARTNERS AND I WANTED TO PUT IN AN APPLIANCE BUSINESS BUT WE COULDN'T FIND A SUITABLE BUILDING.

THERE WAS AN OLD FUNERAL HOME ON ONE OF THE MAIN ROADS IN TOWN WITH A BASEMENT AND A LIFT (ELEVATOR) THAT THEY USED FOR MOVING CASKETS, ETC. FROM THE BASEMENT TO THE MAIN FLOOR UPSTAIRS. IT WAS ALL THAT WAS AVAILABLE AND AFTER A FEW MEETINGS TO DETERMINE HOW TO REMODEL IT WE BOUGHT IT. AFTER DOING SOME WORK ON IT WE HAD A NICE COMMERCIAL BUILDING FOR AN APPLIANCE COMPANY WHICH WAS VERY SUCCESSFUL IN THAT LOCATION. YEARS LATER I ENDED UP SELLING MY SHARE TO ONE OF THE PARTNERS AND TO MY KNOWLEDGE HE IS STILL IN BUSINESS AT THAT LOCATION, AFTER 35 YEARS. LOOKING BACK ON THAT BUILDING – IT COULD HAVE JUST AS EASILY BEEN TURNED INTO A HUGE BEAUTIFUL HOME.

SOME PEOPLE BUY UNOCCUPIED CHURCH BUILDINGS, UNUSED BUILDINGS THAT WERE ONCE A BANK OR SMALL GROCERY STORE AND TURN THEM INTO BEAUTIFUL HOMES. YOU SHOULD ALWAYS KEEP YOUR IMAGINATION WORKING. LOOK, THINK ABOUT THE POSSIBILITIES, BUY IT, FIX IT UP AND MOVE IN.

NOW LET'S GET TO THE MAIN OBJECTIVE OF THIS CHAPTER:

LET'S SAY THAT YOU WANT A HOME THAT HAS AT LEAST 2,400 SQUARE FEET. IF YOU QUALIFY FOR A LOAN BUT YOU DON'T WANT TO LIVE IN AN OLDER HOME WHILE IT IS BEING FIXED UP YOU CAN BUY A NEW SMALL HOME WITH, LET'S SAY 1,200 SQUARE FEET THAT WILL LEAVE YOU WITH EXTRA MONEY EACH MONTH. BE CERTAIN THAT IT FITS YOUR VISION FOR EXPANDING IT SO THAT YOU WILL END UP WITH THE HOME OF YOUR DREAMS. YOU CAN TAKE THE FLOOR PLAN TO AN ARCHITECT TO GET SOME IDEAS OR YOU COULD DRAW UP A SKETCH AND DRAW THE EXPANSION ON COPIES AS MANY TIMES AS NEED BE. IF YOU CAN'T DO IT YOURSELF HAVE A PROFESSIONAL DRAW THE PLANS FOR YOU IN PHASES THAT YOU CAN AFFORD TO PAY STEP BY STEP TO SUB-CONTRACTORS. ONCE THE PLANS ARE APPROVED BY THE TOWN, CITY OR COUNTY YOU WILL BE ABLE TO LOCATE, LET'S SAY, THE PLUMBING CONTRACTOR. DURING THE FIRST MONTH HAVE HIM PUT IN THE UNDERGROUND; THE NEXT MONTH HAVE A CEMENT CONTRACTOR PUT IN THE FOUNDATION; THE NEXT MONTH GET THE FLOORING DONE, ETC. AND PAY FOR IT AS IT IS DONE. YOU WILL BE SURPRISED HOW FAST THAT GOES. OR, SAVE UP SOME MONEY FOR TWO OR THREE MONTHS AND DO ONE STEP. BE SURE TO CALL FOR INSPECTIONS AS REQUIRED BY THE CODE IN YOUR AREA.

BE CERTAIN THAT YOU DO NOT BUY A SMALL HOME IN ONE OF THOSE DEVELOPMENTS OR AREAS WHERE THERE IS A HOME OWNERS ASSOCIATION OR CC&R'S OR RULES THAT CONTROL WHAT YOU DO. THEY PROBABLY WILL NOT LET YOU EXPAND YOUR HOME! IN SOME OF THEM YOU CAN'T EVEN PARK YOUR CAR IN THE DRIVEWAY AT NIGHT – IT HAS

TO BE IN THE GARAGE. YOU CAN'T ALLOW FAMILY OR FRIENDS TO SPEND THE NIGHT IF THEY NEED TO PARK ON THE STREET OR IN THE DRIVEWAY. THERE ARE MANY HORROR STORIES ABOUT THOSE HOME OWNERS ASSOCIATIONS SO WATCH OUT. I SUGGEST THAT YOU BUY ONE THAT DOESN'T HAVE THOSE GROUPS CONTROLING EVERY MOVE YOU MAKE.

YOU CAN JUST BUY LAND AND GET SOME PLANS DRAWN UP FOR YOUR DREAM HOME. HAVE THE ARCHITECT DRAW THEM IN PHASES WHERE YOU CAN BUILD A 1,200 SQUARE FOOT HOUSE AND MOVE INTO IT. THEN FOR PHASE TWO ADD 600 MORE SQUARE FEET AND FOR PHASE THREE ADD ANOTHER 800 SQUARE FEET OR WHATEVER FITS YOUR NEEDS.

AFTER THE FIRST PHASE IS COMPLETE YOU ARE NOW LIVING IN YOUR OWN HOME AND NOT THROWING AWAY ANY MONEY ON RENT. WITH THE MONEY YOU SAVE YOU CAN START ON THE NEXT PHASE AND SO ON.

I BUILT A 2,600 SQUARE FOOT HOUSE OVER A PERIOD OF SIX YEARS WITH A BUDGET THAT I COULD AFFORD EACH MONTH AND DO NOT OWE ONE DOLLAR ON IT. I STARTED WITH A 1,600 SQUARE FOOT HOUSE BUT I DIDN'T RESTRICT IT WITH A LOT OF INTERIOR WALLS. I BUILT IT WITH ONLY ONE WALL SEPERATING THE MAIN HOME FROM THE BEDROOM – BATH – LAUNDRY – CLOSET AREA. LATER I WILL BE ABLE TO SIMPLY ADD A NON SUPPORTING WALL HERE OR THERE TO DIVIDE IT AS WANTED. I THEN ADDED ON 1,000 SQUARE FEET DURING PHASE TWO AS TWO MORE BEDROOMS – A BATH – A LAUNDRY ROOM – AND, AN OFFICE. I AM NOW ADDING ON ANOTHER 800 SQUARE FEET FOR PHASE THREE AND I WILL END UP WITH A 3,400 SQUARE FOOT HOME THAT IS PAID FOR WITH NO MORTGAGE PAYMENTS. TOTAL TIME MAY BE TEN YEARS BUT IT IS MINE AND IT IS PAID FOR! HEY, I MAY NOT BE DONE YET! MY NEW WIFE, MONICA, WANTS MORE SPACE SO I AM DRAWING PLANS FOR PHASE FOUR WHICH WILL ADD ANOTHER 600 SQUARE FEET TO OUR HOME. WE WILL END UP WITH A 4,000 SQUARE FOOT MANSION WORTH A MILLION OR MORE WHICH IS LOCATED ALMOST UP AGAINST THE MOUNTAINS WITH A VIEW OF THE ENTIRE VALLEY AND THE LIGHTS OF THE NEW CITY THAT IS BEING BUILT, AS YOU READ THIS, IN THE VALLEY ABOUT TEN MILES AWAY.

WHEN I MET MONICA I WAS LIVING IN THE 1600 SQUARE FOOT HOME THAT I HAD BUILT AND I HAD ALSO DRAWN UP THE PLANS THAT WOULD ALLOW ME TO ADD ON 1,000 SQUARE FEET FOR PHASE TWO BUT SINCE I WAS SINGLE, I WASN'T IN A HURRY. NOW THAT I AM MARRIED MY MOTIVATION TO FINISH THE HOME IS REJUVENATED SO MORE WORK IS UNDERWAY. YOU CAN DO IT TOO! ALL YOU NEED IS SOME LAND!

LAND DIRT CHEAP

YOU JUST READ ABOUT THE HOME I HAVE BEEN BUILDING IN THE LAST CHAPTER SO I WILL TELL YOU A LITTLE ABOUT HOW THAT HAPPENED.

I WAS LIVING IN PHOENIX AND IT WAS ONE OF THOSE TIMES THAT I WAS RENTING A HOUSE. I WORKED LONG HOURS AT LEAST SIX DAYS A WEEK AND THE RENTAL WAS CLOSE TO WORK SO I JUST DIDN'T TAKE THE TIME TO LOOK FOR SOMETHING TO BUY FOR OVER A YEAR. WHEN I DID START LOOKING I WANTED SOMETHING WITH POTENTIAL AND IN THE PATH OF FUTURE GROWTH. EXPERIENCE HAD TAUGHT ME WHAT TO LOOK FOR AND WHAT I WANTED: LAND WITH A VIEW, CLOSE TO MOUNTAINS, CLOSE TO STATE OR FEDERAL LAND FOR HORSES OR FOUR WHEELING, HIKING AND OPEN SPACE, SOME NEW CONSTRUCTION IN PROGRESS AND AT A PRICE THAT SHOULD ALLOW THE LAND TO INCREASE IN VALUE. IT SHOULD HAVE ELECTRICITY AND WATER AT THE VERY LEAST AND REASONABLE ACCESS. I FOUND SIX ACRES SOUTH OF MARICOPA WHICH IS SOUTH OF PHOENIX THAT FIT MY REQUIREMENTS AND HAD A BEAUTIFUL VIEW SO I BOUGHT IT; MOVED A MOBILE HOME ON IT, PUT IN A SEPTIC SYSTEM, PAID USWEST AT THE TIME TO RUN PHONE LINES FROM ½ MILE AWAY, HOOKED UP WATER AND ELECTRIC AND MOVED IN; THEN IT WAS SPLIT INTO LOTS AND I IMPROVED EACH OF THEM; AND STARTED BUILDING MY HOME.

THE FIRST THING YOU WILL NEED TO DO IS LOCATE SOME LAND THAT YOU LIKE AND PURCHASE IT WITH A LOW DOWN PAYMENT, LOW PAYMENTS AND IF POSSIBLE LOW INTEREST – UNLESS YOU CAN PAY CASH FOR IT. YOU COULD USE THE INFORMATION CONTAINED IN THIS BOOK TO NEGOTIATE WHEN YOU ARE BUYING AND YOU SHOULD TALK TO PROFESSIONALS SUCH AS TITLE COMPANIES, REAL ESTATE AGENTS, ATTORNEYS AND THE LEGAL ENTITY THAT ISSUES PERMITS FOR DIVIDING LAND AND BUILDING PERMITS.

YOU MAY NEED TO STAY WHERE YOU LIVE NOW IF YOU CAN AFFORD IT WHILE YOU ARE BUILDING A SUITABLE PLACE TO LIVE ON YOUR LAND OR DOWN SIZE SO THAT YOU CAN AFFORD TO BUY LAND AND START ON YOUR WAY TO WEALTH. BUT, AFTER ALL, YOU ARE A WORKING MAN OR WOMAN, RIGHT? YOU'RE STILL YOUNG, SELL SOME MORE TIME! IT ONLY TAKES A FEW YEARS AND YOU CAN BECOME WEALTHY LONG BEFORE MOST PEOPLE WILL. YOU CAN BECOME WEALTHY AT AN AGE WHERE YOU CAN STILL ENJOY LIFE. MOST PEOPLE WORK ALL OF THEIR LIFE JUST TO OWN A HOME THAT IS PAID FOR AND IF THEY'RE LUCKY THEY WILL HAVE A FEW DOLLARS FOR RETIREMENT TO SUPPLEMENT THEIR SOCIAL SECURITY. DON'T BE LIKE THAT! BECOME WEALTHY!

WHAT DO YOU WANT OUT OF THE LAND YOU ARE LOOKING FOR? VIEWS, MOUNTAINS, MAIN ROADS, NO NEIGHBORS, BACK ROADS, PRIVACY, DIVIDEABLE INTO LOTS, UTILITIES, SECURITY, OR? FIND THE LAND THAT YOU LIKE AND INVESTIGATE IT TO MAKE CERTAIN IT FITS YOUR FUTURE PLANS. ONCE YOU HAVE FOUND IT NEGOTIATE AND BUY IT AND YOUR NEW HOME CAN BECOME A VERY PROFITABLE REALITY AND YOU CAN'T LOSE IT, IF YOU LOSE YOUR JOB.

THE NECESSITIES AND A SHELTER

MOST OF US NEED SOME CREATURE COMFORTS SUCH AS WATER, ELECTRIC AND SEWER, OF COURSE, AND WE ALSO NEED A SHELTER. YOU AND YOUR FAMILY HAVE TO DECIDE WHAT YOUR MINIMUM REQUIREMENTS ARE.

CAN YOU GET BY IN A CABIN, A SMALL HOUSE, A MOBILE HOME OR SOMETHING OTHER THAN WHAT YOU REALLY WANT FOR A LITTLE WHILE? SURE YOU CAN BUT YOU HAVE TO REALLY WANT TO DO IT.

BECOMING WEALTHY BY OWNING YOUR OWN HOME WITHOUT A DEBT ON IT CAN BECOME AN ADVENTURE FOR YOU, YOUR SPOUSE AND THE KIDS. GET EVERYONE INVOLVED AND LET THEM TELL YOU WHAT THEY WANT THEIR ROOM TO LOOK LIKE, WHAT THEY WANT THE YARD TO LOOK LIKE AND ANYTHING ELSE THAT WILL GET THEM EXCITED ABOUT THE ADVENTURE. DRAW SKETCHES, LET THEM DRAW SKETCHES AND DISCUSS ALL OF IT AFTER DINNER. IT JUST MAY BE POSSIBLE, IF ALL OF YOU WORK TOGETHER AS A FAMILY, THAT YOU MAY BE ABLE TO DO THIS AND YOU MAY HELP YOUR KIDS BREAK AWAY FROM SHAKEY FRIENDS OR BAD HABITS OR EVEN ADDICTIONS. TAKE A BREAK EVERY MONTH FOR A WEEK-END AND DO SOMETHING TOGETHER THAT YOU ALL ENJOY SUCH AS A THEME PARK, A SHORT TRIP OR HIKEING TO KEEP FROM GETTING BURNED OUT, ESPECIALLY IF IT IS A TWO OR THREE YEAR PROJECT. SOMETIMES IMPATIENCE AND LOST INTEREST KILLS THE PLAN RIGHT IN THE MIDDLE – DON'T LET THAT HAPPEN – KEEP UP THE EXCITEMENT AND THINK POSITIVE. DON'T FORGET WILLING FAMILY AND FRIENDS BUT BE SURE TO RETURN THE FAVOR WHEN THEY START THEIR HOME ON THE PROPERTY NEXT DOOR.

THERE ARE MANY OPTIONS FOR YOU. USE ONE OF THEM – STOP THROWING AWAY YOUR HARD EARNED MONEY ON RENT!

PICK YOUR FUTURE HOME

YOU MAY BE ABLE TO PICK YOUR FUTURE HOME BY LOOKING AT A HOME THAT IS ALREADY BUILT. GO LOOK AT NEW HOMES IN NEW DEVELOPMENTS AND GET A COPY OF THE FLOOR PLAN THAT YOU LIKE. DON'T LET THE SALESMAN AND TEMPTATION TAKE HOLD AND TALK YOU INTO BUYING ONE THOUGH. IF YOU NEED TO YOU CAN TAKE THE FLOOR PLAN TO A DRAFTSMAN AND HAVE HIM OR HER DRAW ONE SIMILAR – IN PHASES – FOR YOU TO START WITH AND YOU CAN ADD ON ADDITIONAL LIVING SPACE LATER.

IN MOST STATES YOU CAN BE YOUR OWN CONTRACTOR. TAKE THE PLANS FOR YOUR NEW HOME AND GET THEM APPROVED BY THE LOCAL AUTHORITY. ONCE THEY HAVE BEEN APPROVED YOU WILL BE ABLE TO START STEP BY STEP AND CONTACT A SUB-CONTRACTOR TO DO THE GROUND WORK IN PREPARATION FOR YOUR HOME IF IT IS BEYOND YOU TO COMPLETE THAT STEP. THE ARCHITECT WILL ACTUALLY BE ABLE TO GIVE YOU A LIST OF STEPS TO BUILD A HOME. IF THERE ARE ANY OF THE STEPS THAT YOU, WITH THE HELP OF FAMILY AND FRIENDS, CAN DO, YOU SHOULD DO THAT STEP YOURSELF AND SAVE THE WASTED LABOR COST. IN THE LONG RUN YOU ARE NOT ONLY SAVING MONEY BUT YOU ARE GETTING PAID FOR EVERY HOUR YOU SPEND ON THE WORK BY ACCUMULATING EQUITY AT NO ACTUAL COST.

GO AHEAD. LOOK AT NEW HOMES; LOOK AT PLAN BOOKS WHICH ARE AVAILABLE AT HOME DEPOT OR LOWES AND PICK OUT WHAT YOUR FUTURE HOME WILL LOOK LIKE.

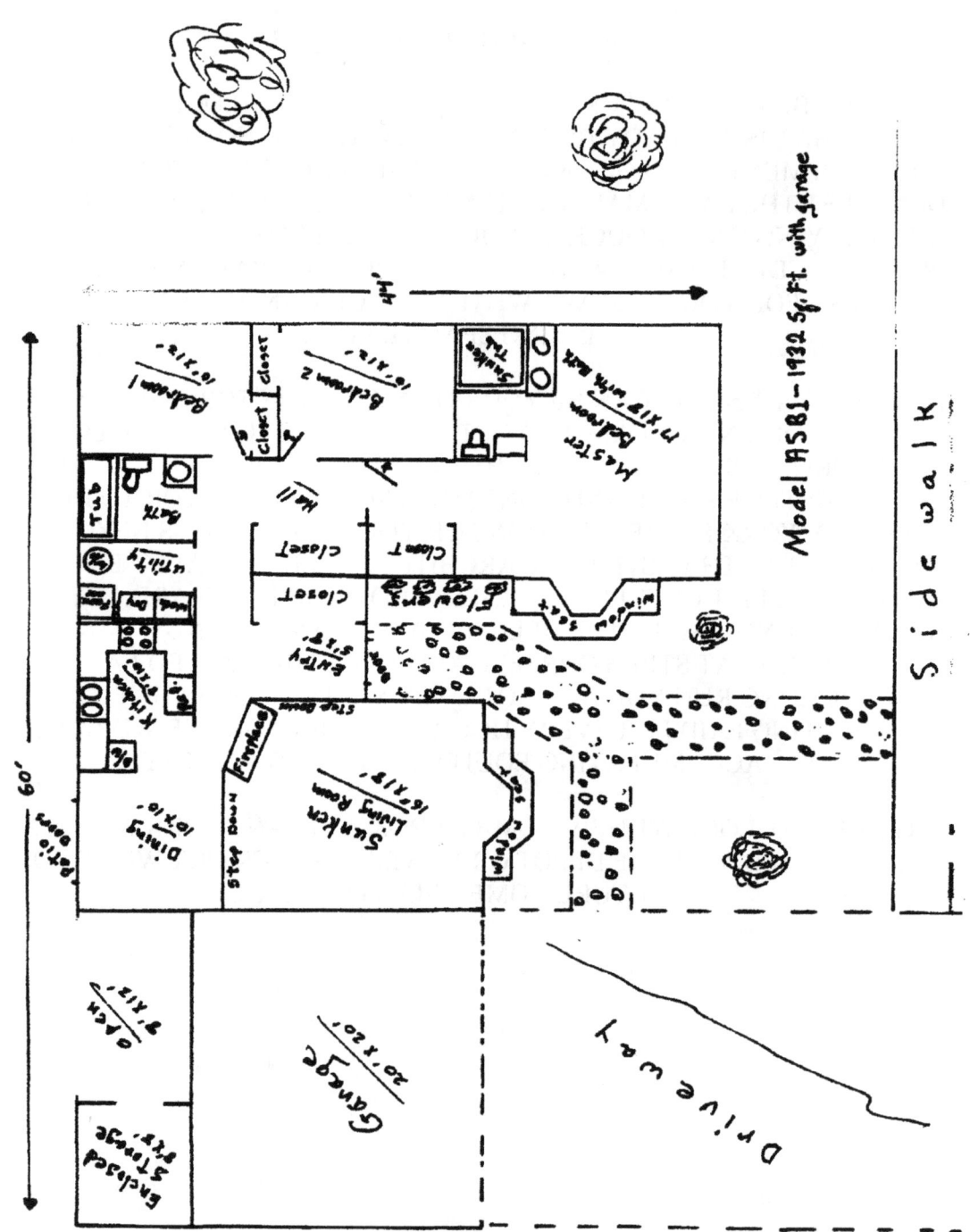

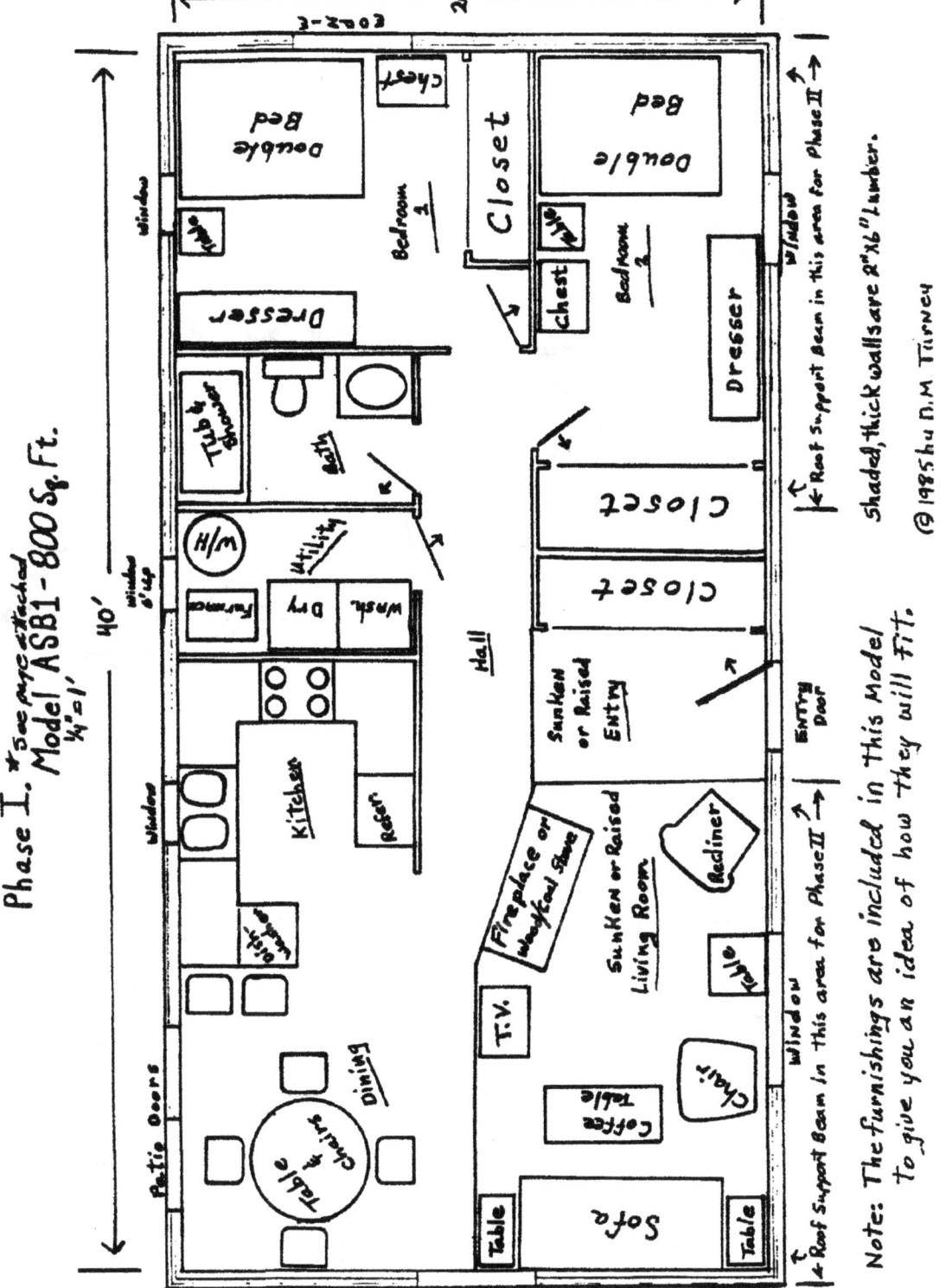

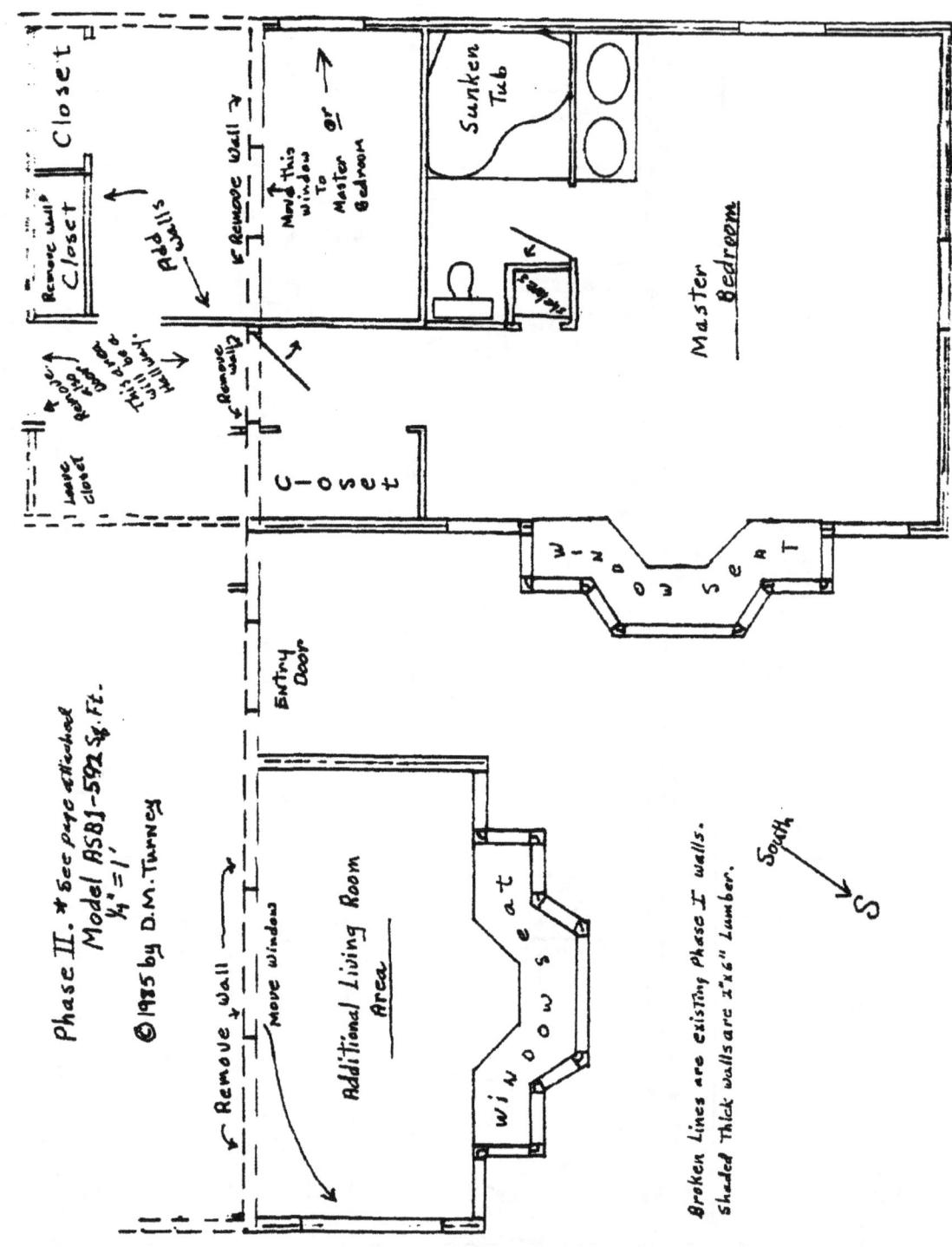

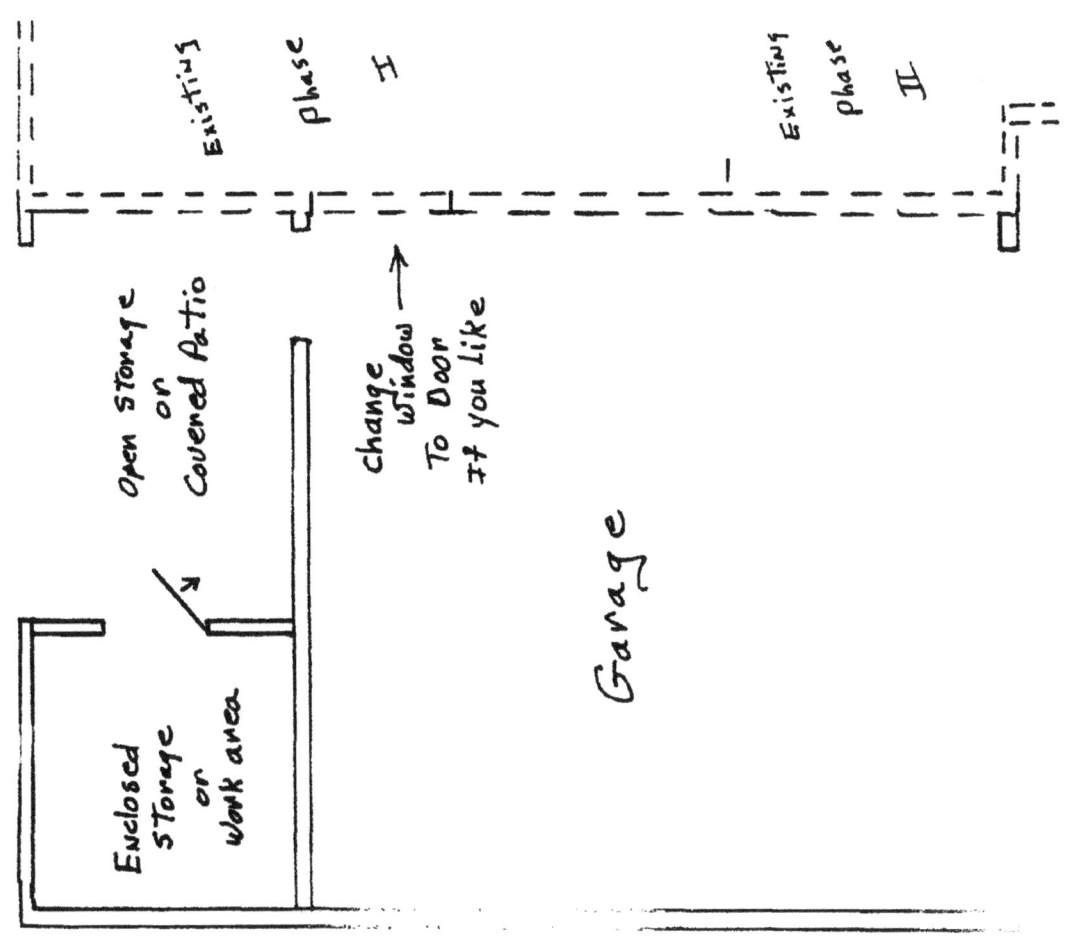

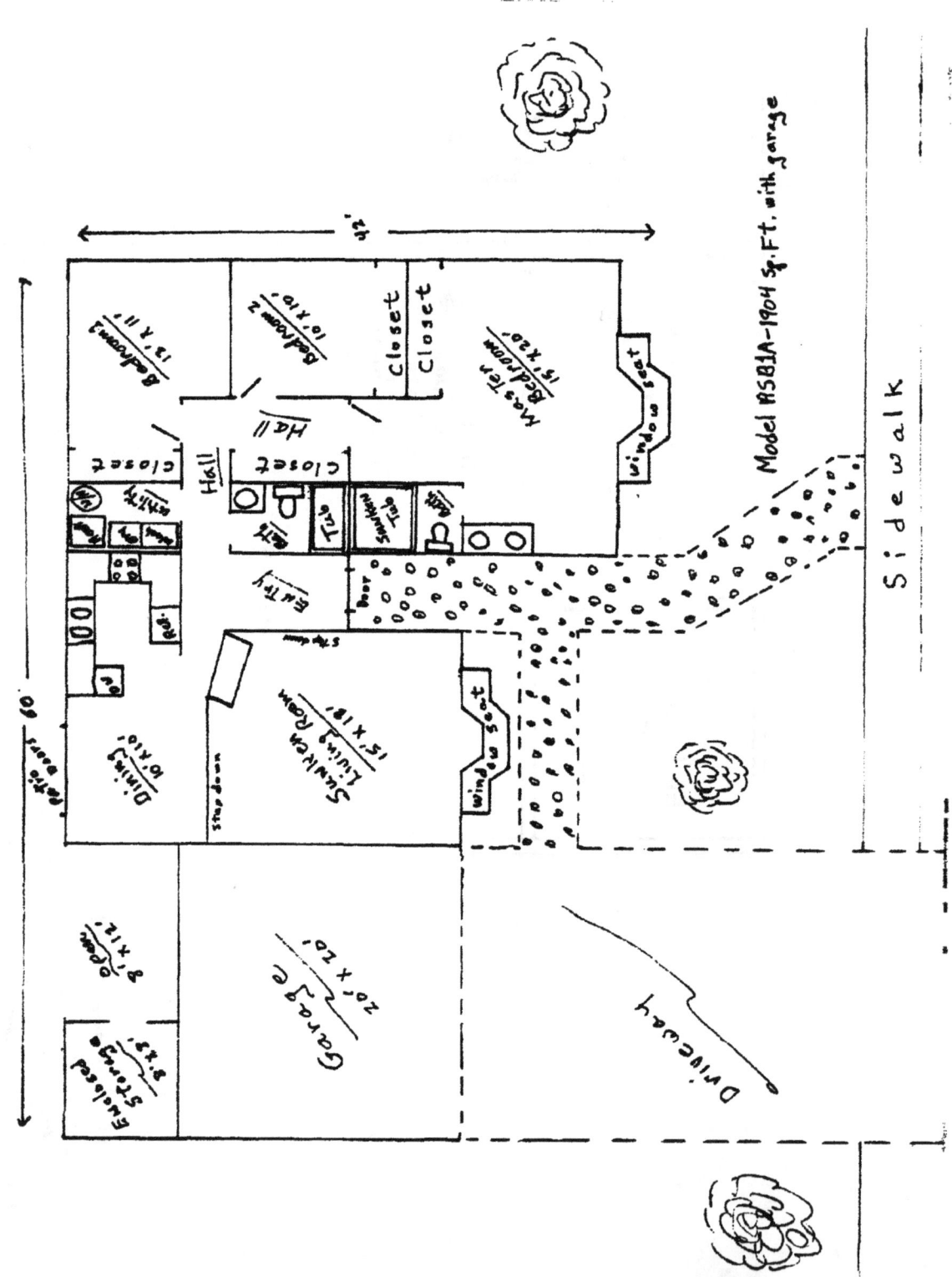

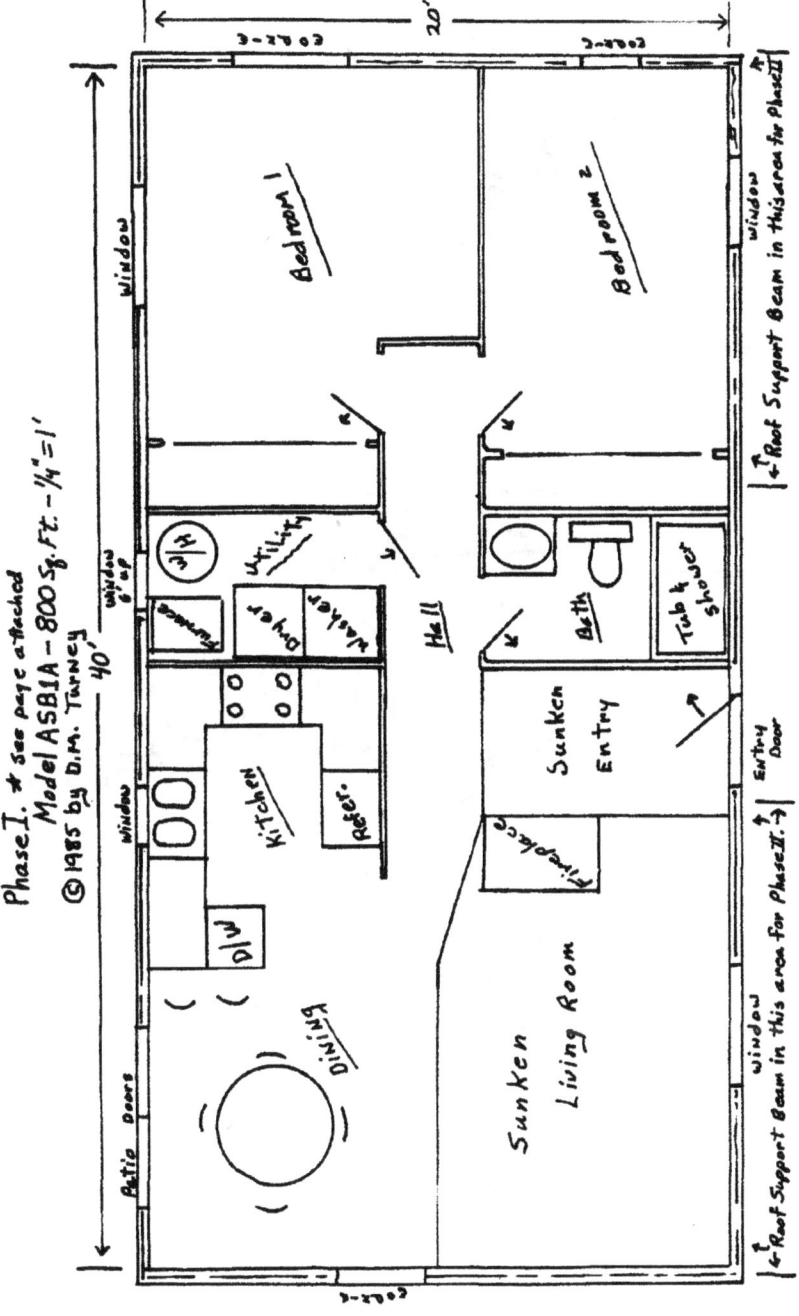

Phase II

*See Page attached

Model ASB1A – 564 Sq. Ft.

© 1985 by D.M. Tunney

Broken Lines are existing Phase I walls.
Shaded thick walls are 2"x6" Lumber.

Note: For Phase III see Phase III for Model ASB1.

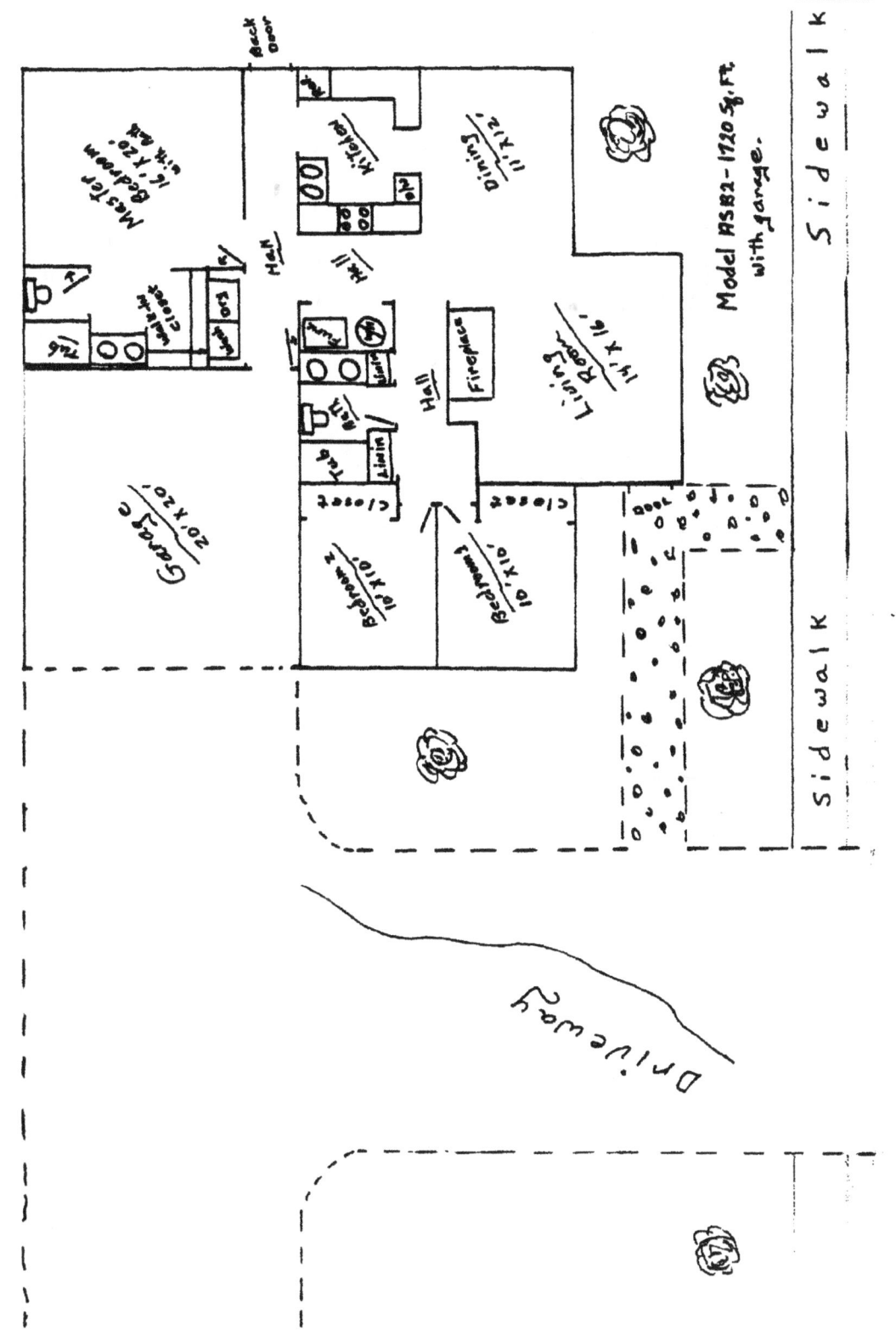

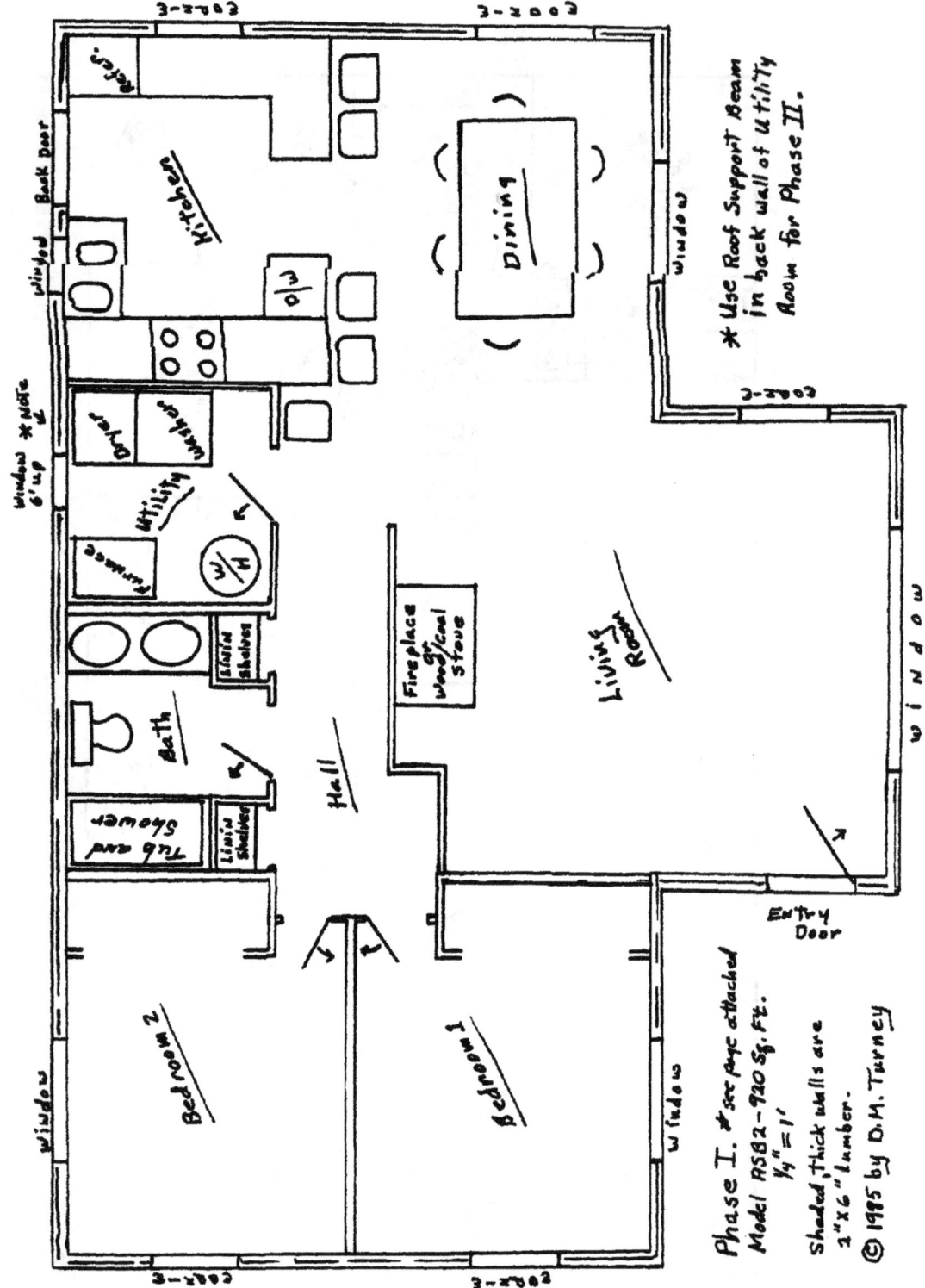

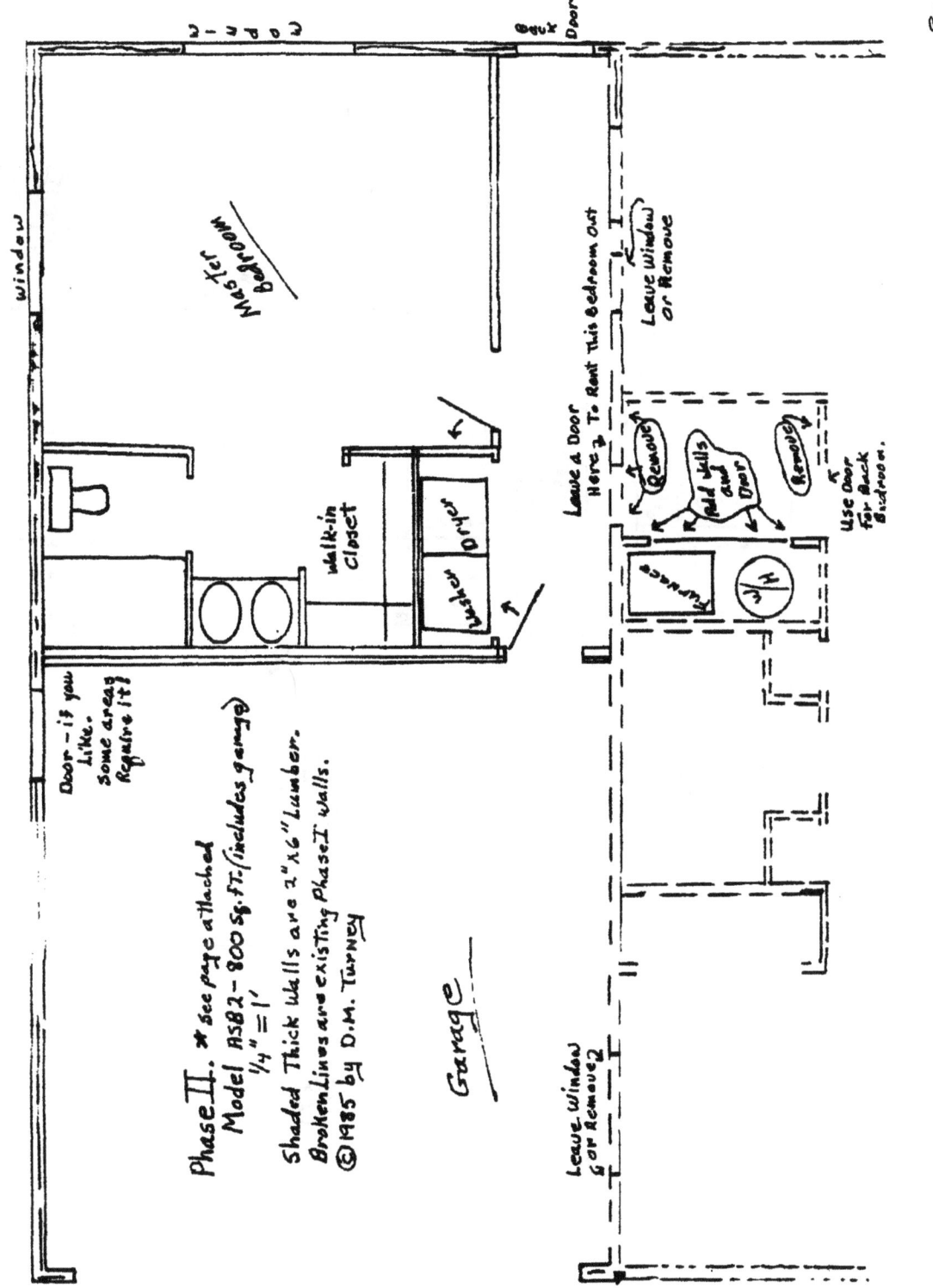

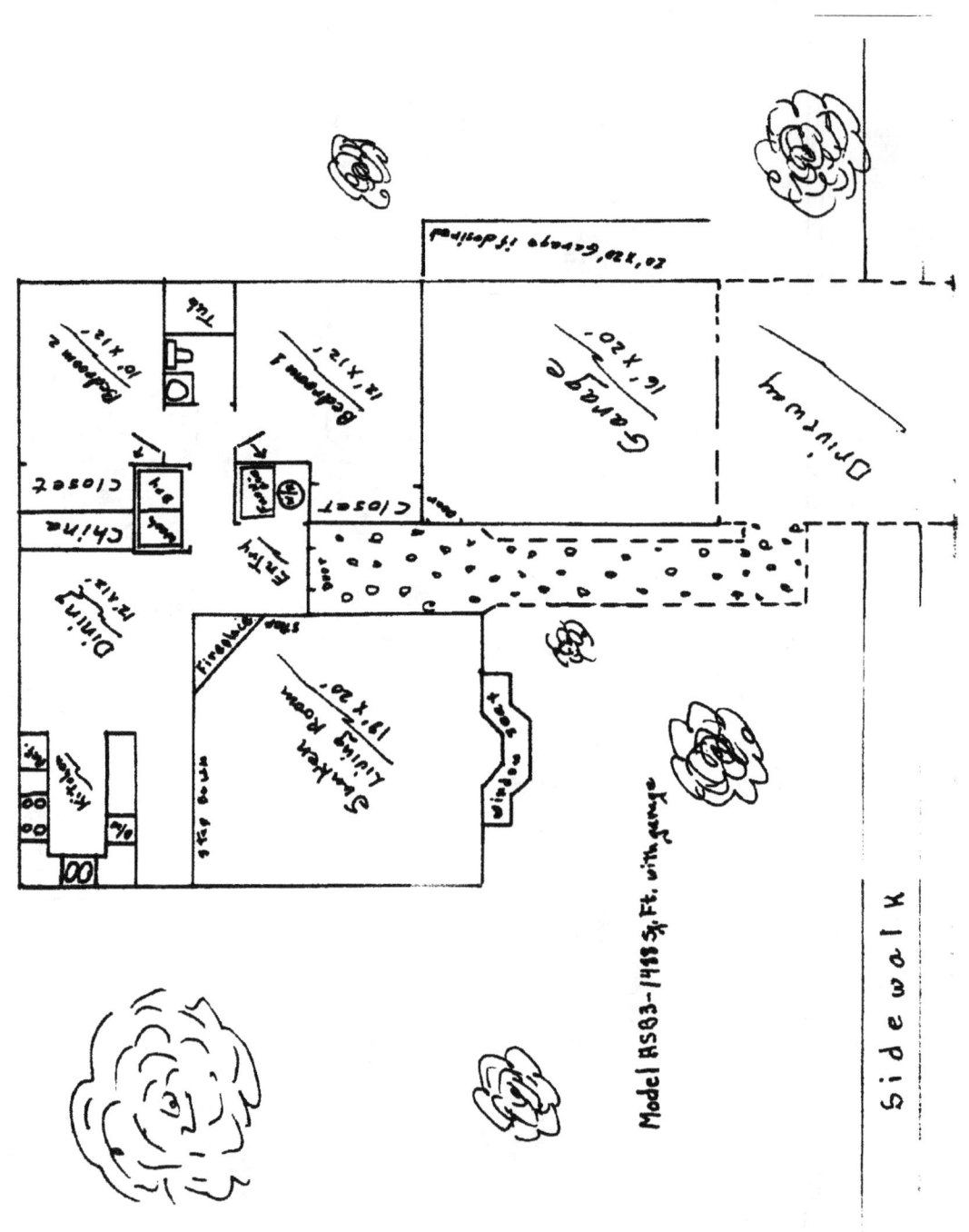

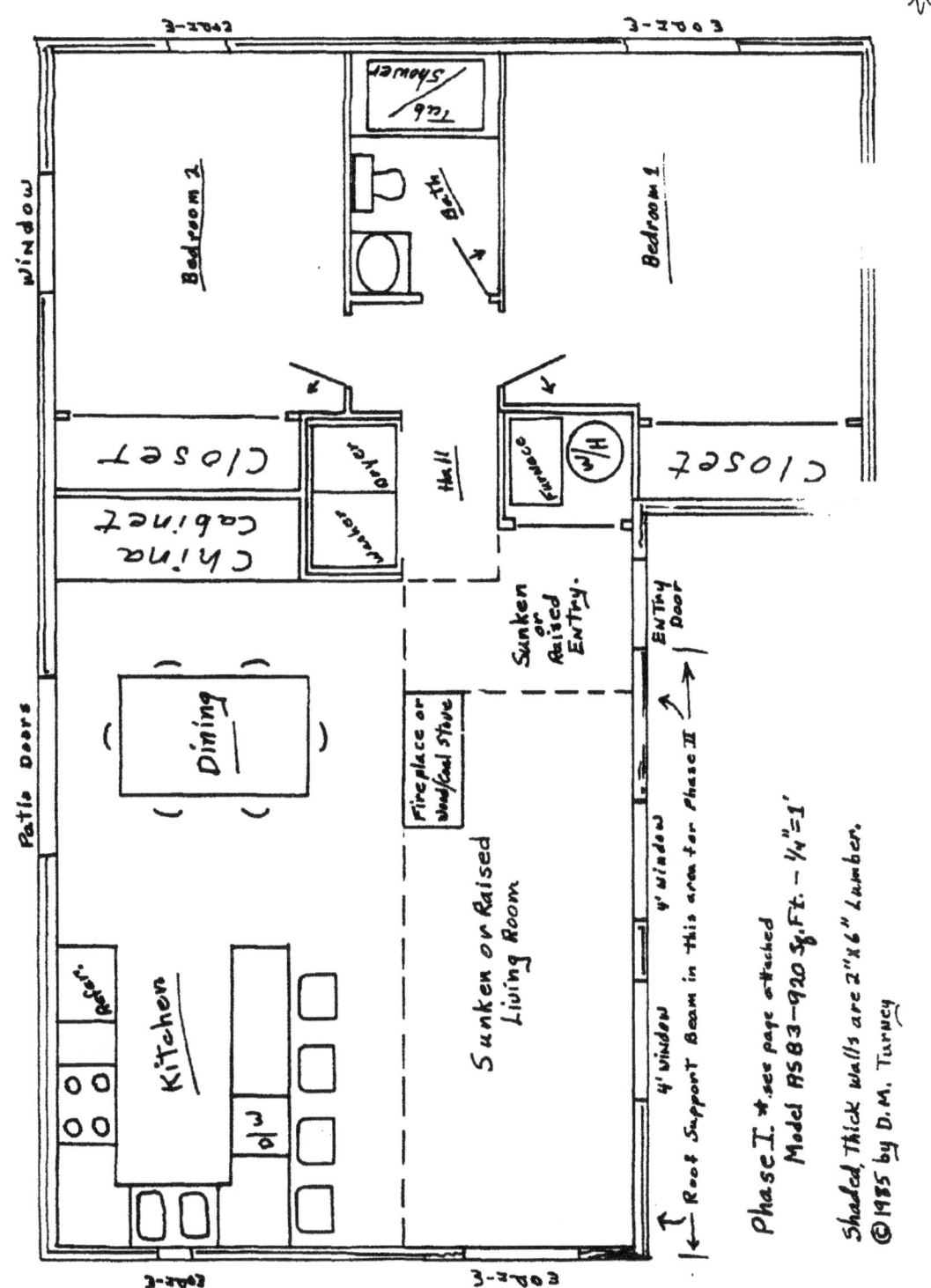

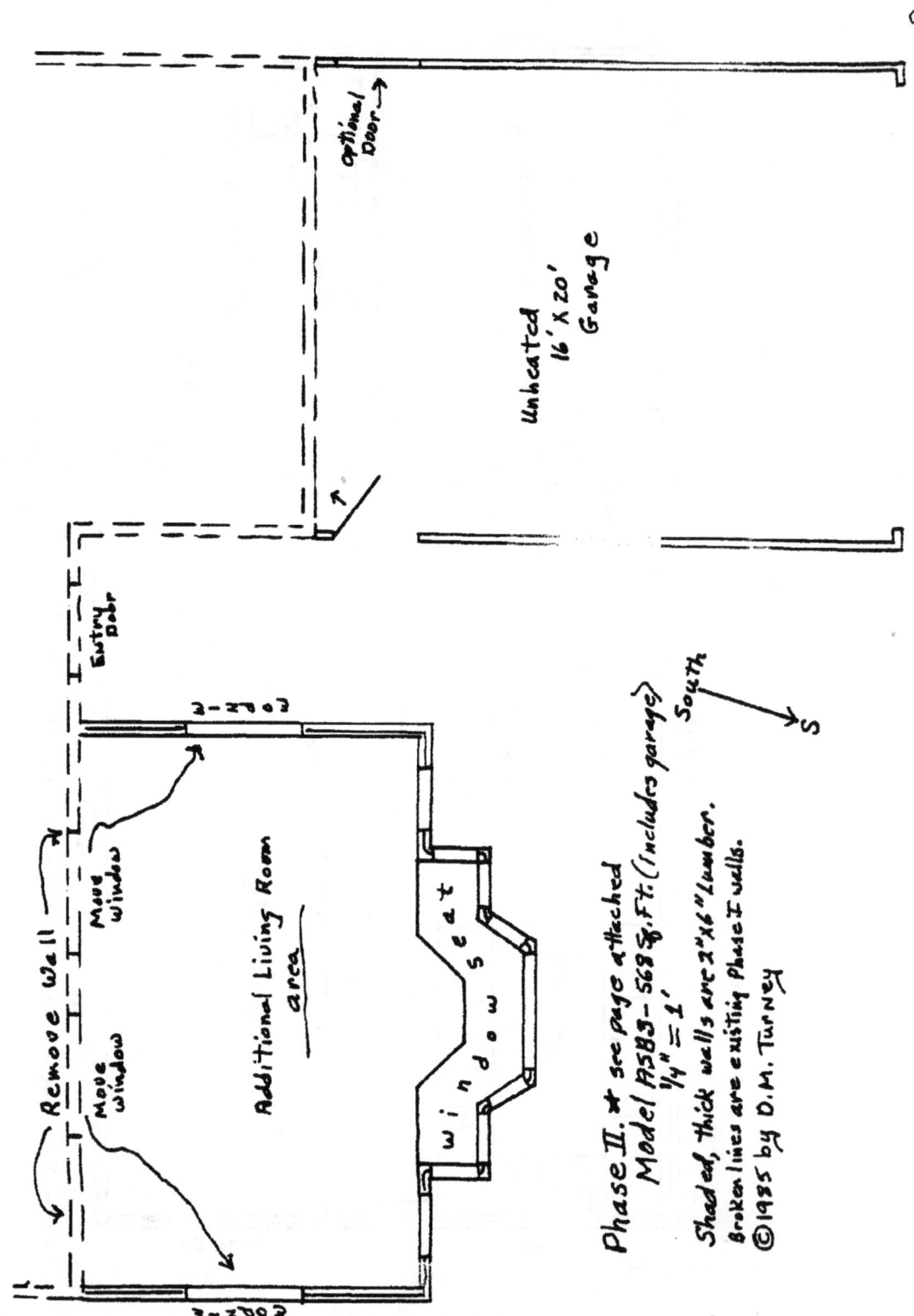

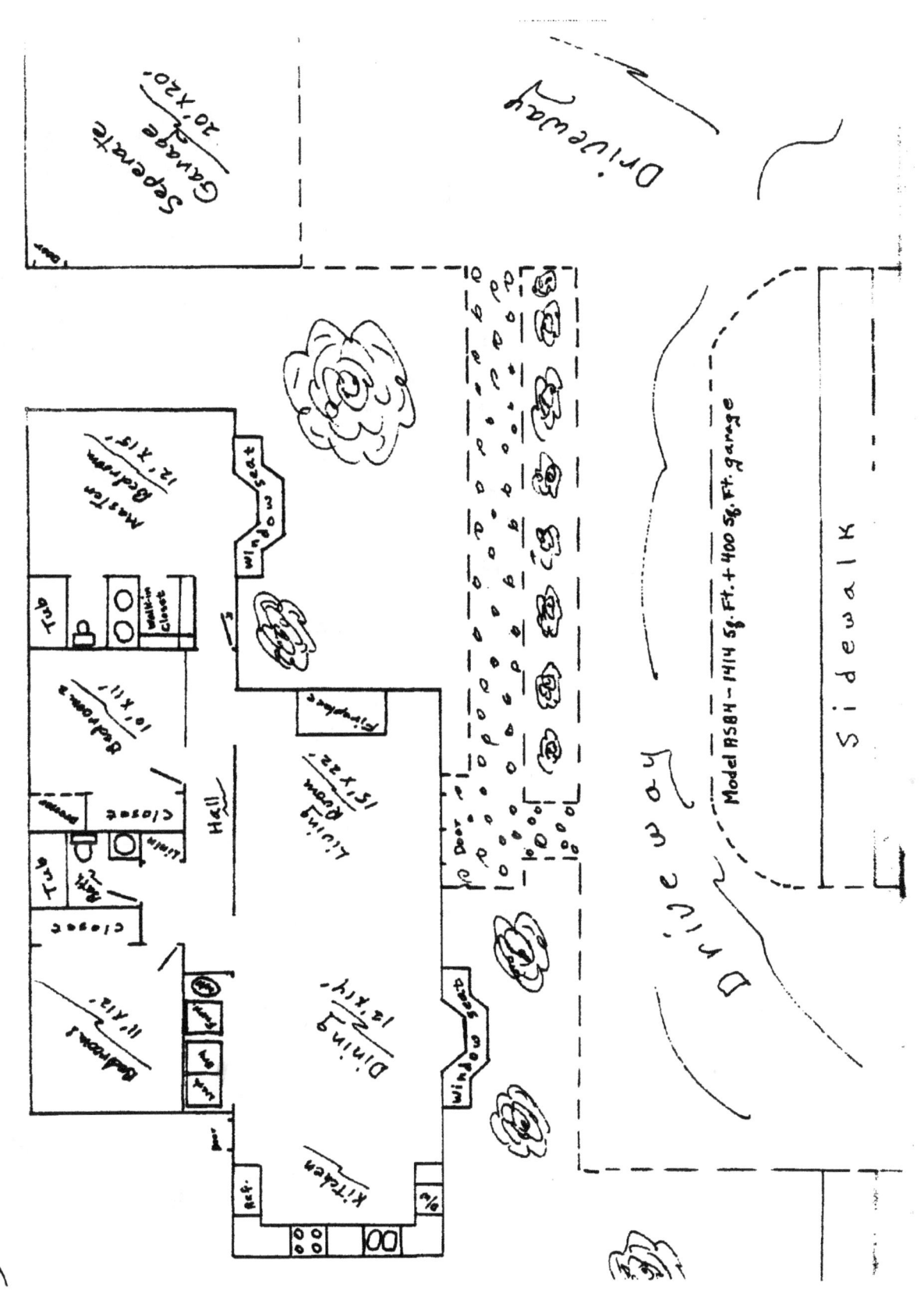

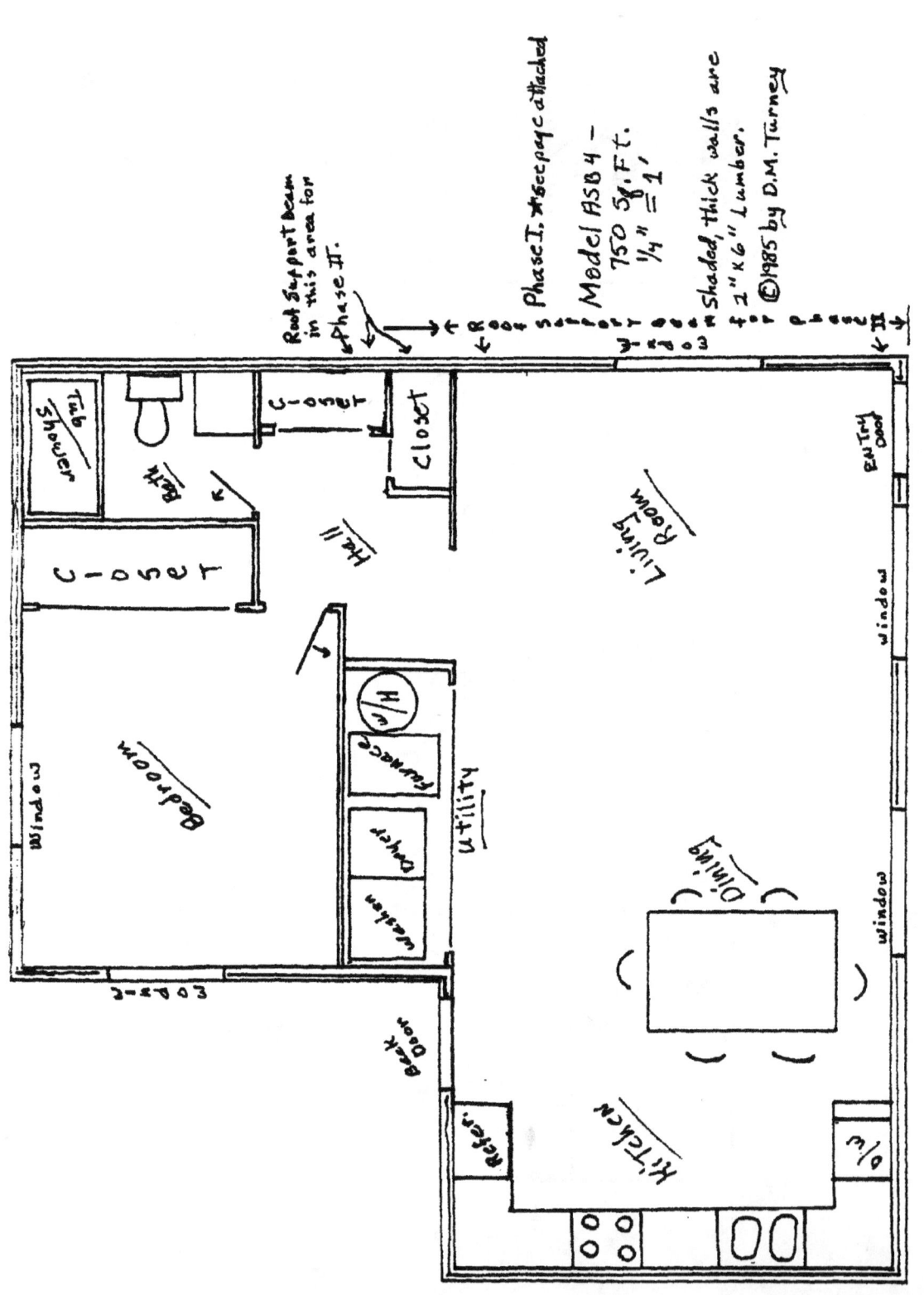

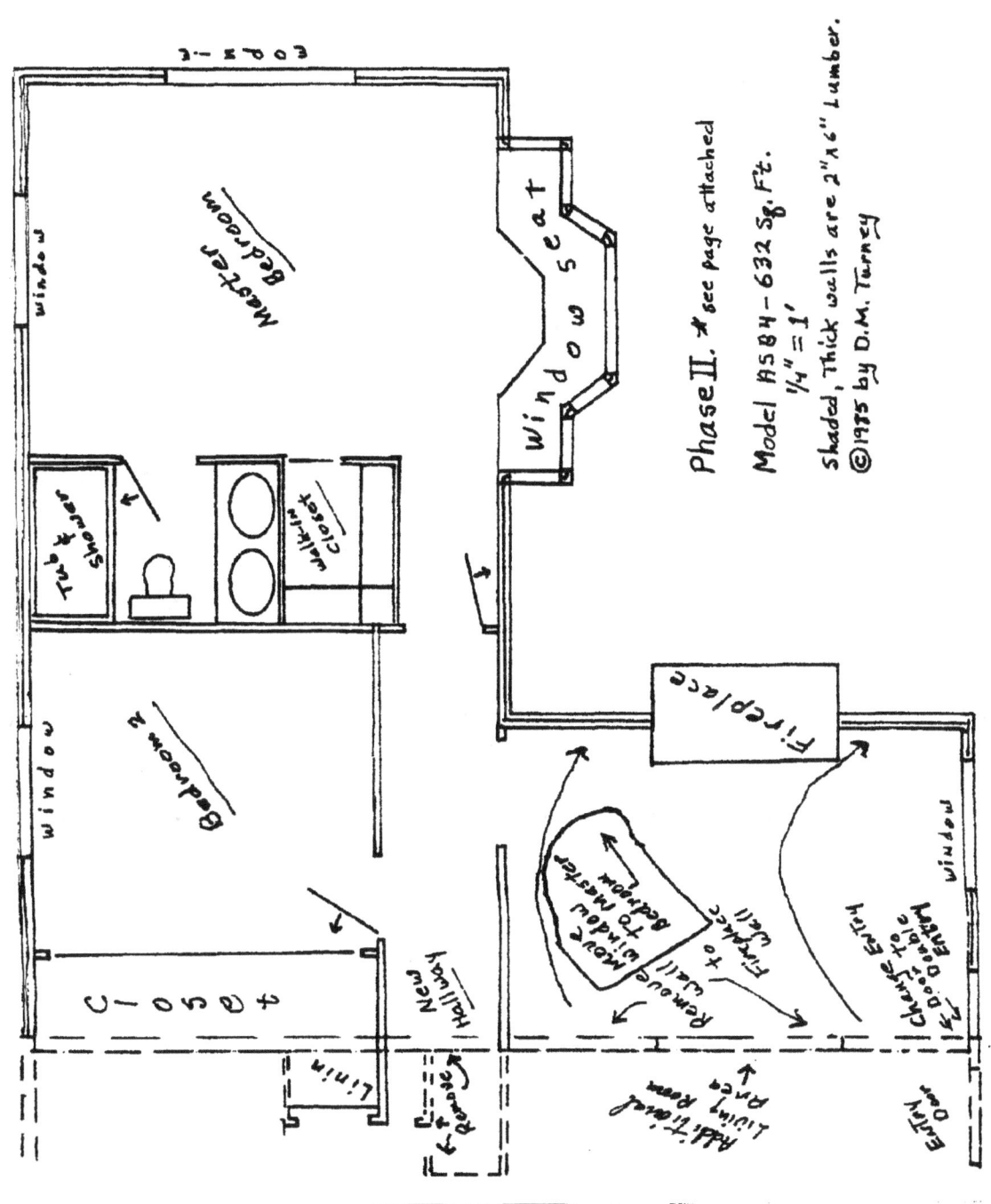

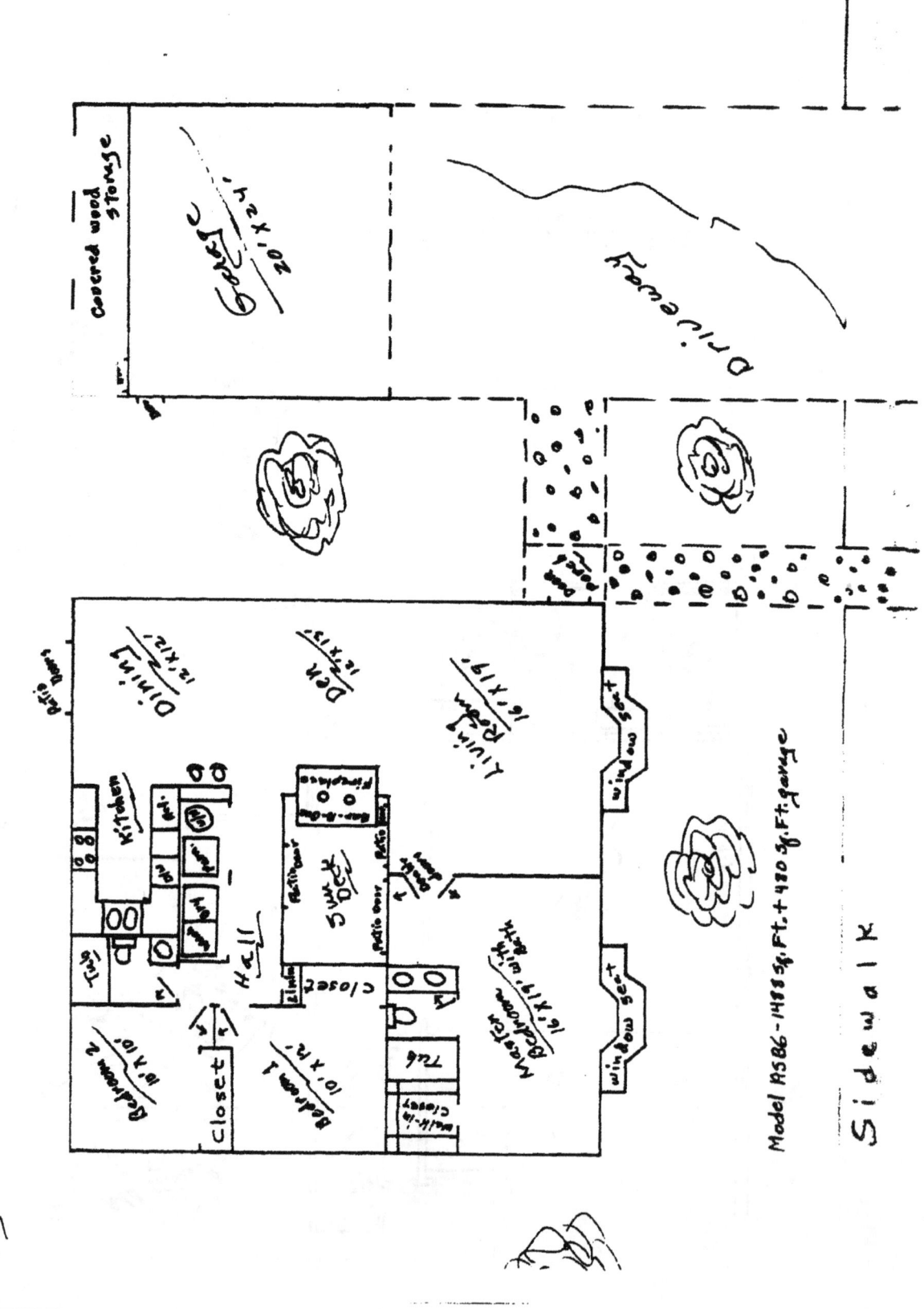

YOU CAN PLAN YOUR OWN HOME

AS YOU CAN SEE ON THE PRIOR PAGES THERE ISN'T ANY BIG SECRETS TO SKETCHING YOUR OWN PLANS. ONCE YOU HAVE A REASONABLY GOOD SKETCH YOU CAN HAVE A DRAFTSMAN OR ARCHITECT PUT THEM IN A FORM WHERE YOU WILL BE ABLE TO USE THEM TO GET A PERMIT. ONCE THIS IS DONE ANY CONTRACTORS WILL BE ABLE TO WORK FROM THEM. BE SURE TO GET SEVERAL COPIES – ONE FOR THE GROUND WORK, ONE FOR THE PLUMBER, ONE FOR THE CEMENT CONTRACTOR, ONE FOR THE FRAMER, THE ELECTRICIAN, ETC. YOU AND YOUR FAMILY CAN COME UP WITH YOUR DREAM HOME SO GO AHEAD SIT DOWN TOGETHER AND MAKE SOME SKETCHES. THERE IS A LOT OF SATISFACTION IN PLANNING YOUR OWN HOME AND WORKING TOGETHER ON IT AS A FAMILY!

THINGS TO KEEP IN MIND

LEAVE ROOM IN THE BATHS SO THAT YOU CAN TOWEL OFF IN COMFORT AND DOUBLE SINKS IF YOU WANT; LEAVE ROOM AROUND THE TOILET SO THAT LARGE FAMILY MEMBERS CAN SIT IN COMFORT; LEAVE THE DOOR OPENINGS LARGE ENOUGH TO GET FURNITURE IN AND OUT; PLAN THE CLOSETS; PLAN THE SPACE FOR LAUNDRY, FURNACE, AIR CONDITIONING, WATER HEATER, ETC.; PLAN THE KITCHEN CABINETS; PLAN THE WINDOWS THAT YOU WANT IN YOUR NEW HOME; TALK TO YOUR LOCAL SUPPLY HOUSES SUCH AS HOME DEPOT OR LOWES. THEY WILL HELP YOU WITH PLANNING A LOT OF YOUR NEW HOME SO BE CERTAIN TO ASK. THEY WILL EVEN GIVE YOU A MATERIAL LIST, PLANNING SHEET TO ALLOW YOU TO LAY OUT YOUR KITCHEN, SPRINKLER SYSTEM AND MORE AND THEY WILL QUOTE PRICES FOR EACH PHASE OF YOUR ADVENTURE.

IF YOU CAN'T DO IT YOURSELF WORK WITH YOUR ARCHITECT (THEY'RE ACTUALLY REASONABLE IN PRICE) AND PLAN IT IN PHASES AT A REAL BUDGET THAT YOU CAN AFFORD.

KEEP IN MIND WHILE YOU ARE PLANNING YOUR HOME, WHILE YOU ARE BUILDING YOUR HOME AND WHILE YOU ARE EXPANDING YOUR HOME THAT YOU MUST FOLLOW THE BUILDING CODES FOR THAT AREA AND HAVE EACH STEP INSPECTED. IT IS NOT THAT DIFFICULT AND YOU CAN ALWAYS USE PROFESSIONALS FOR THE STEPS THAT YOU CANNOT DO.

IT TAKES A LITTLE EFFORT

ONE OF THE THINGS YOU CAN DO IS SELL SOME OF YOUR TIME BY TAKING A PART TIME JOB AS A HELPER AT ONE OF THE CONSTRUCTION JOBS CLOSE TO HOME. YOU CAN HELP AS A LABORER FOR A WHILE THEN WORK AS A PLUMBERS HELPER OR A FRAMERS HELPER. IN JUST A YEAR OR SO OF HELPING YOU WILL BE SURPRISED AT WHAT YOU CAN DO.

AS YOU HAVE NO DOUBT NOTICED, EVERYTHING IN THIS BOOK REQUIRES AN EFFORT ON YOUR PART – WORK, BUT THAT'S WHY YOU BOUGHT THIS BOOK IN THE FIRST PLACE – THE WORKING MAN AND WOMANS WAY TO WEALTH – BECAUSE YOU DON'T MIND A LITTLE WORK. THAT IS THE AMERICAN WAY! OUR ANCESTORS WORKED HARD FOR WHAT THEY GOT – THIS COUNTRY WAS BUILT ON HARD WORK. BESIDES, THERE IS NOT A LAZY WAY TO GET RICH OR A WAY YOU CAN JUST THINK YOURSELF RICH! THERE IS A WORKING WAY AND WE KNOW THAT. TO BECOME WEALTHY TAKES WORK AND SINCE YOU ARE WILLING TO DO THAT YOU CAN DO IT – YOU CAN BECOME WEALTHY – WITH EFFORT.

LET ME TELL YOU A LITTLE STORY. WHEN I WAS A CHILD THERE WAS AN OLD MAN – TO ME AT THE TIME – WHO WAS PROBABLY IN HIS 60'S THAT BOUGHT SOME LAND ACROSS THE ROAD FROM US. WE CALLED HIM "GRANDPA ROGERS". HIS LAST NAME WAS ROGERS. I BELIEVE HE HAD RETIRED BUT AS WAS COMMON AT THAT TIME HE HAD GROWN ACCUSTOMED TO HARD WORK. HE WASN'T WEALTHY BY ANY MEANS BUT HE WASN'T BROKE EITHER.

I NOTICED THAT HE DIVIDED THE LAND INTO LOTS AND HIRED A COUPLE GUYS TO HELP HIM WHO HAD SOME EXPERIENCE IN BUILDING HOMES AND THEY WENT TO WORK BUILDING A HOUSE ON ONE OF THE LOTS. HE LIVED SOMEWHERE ELSE IN THE TOWN WHERE WE LIVED BUT HE WOULD SHOW UP AT SUN UP FOR WORK EVERY DAY AND SO WOULD HIS HELPERS. I WOULD GO OVER EVERY ONCE IN AWHILE WHEN I HAD TIME AFTER THE CHORES POPPA HAD ME DOING AND WOULD OFFER TO HELP. HE WOULD LET ME CLEAN UP OR DO THINGS THAT A NINE YEAR OLD COULD DO AND WOULD GIVE ME FIFTY CENTS OR A DOLLAR FOR MY WORK WHICH I THOUGHT WAS GREAT. WHEN HE GOT DONE WITH THE FIRST HOME HE SOLD IT AND THEN HE STARTED ANOTHER ONE ON ANOTHER LOT ALL BY HIMSELF. WHEN HE GOT DONE WITH IT HE AND HIS WIFE MOVED INTO IT AND HE STILL HAD TWO LOTS LEFT. SEVERAL YEARS LATER, AFTER I GOT OUT OF THE MILITARY, I WENT BACK TO WHERE WE HAD LIVED AT THAT TIME AND GRANDPA ROGERS HAD BUILT TWO MORE HOUSES ON THE

EMPTY LOTS AND SOLD THEM OR HAD THEM RENTED OUT. HE WAS MUCH OLDER BUT STILL ALIVE AND STILL ACTIVE.

GRANDPA ROGER HAD WORK ETHICS, WAS SELF DISCIPLINED AND MOTIVATED. IT APPEARED TO ME THAT HE LEARNED A LOT FROM THE TWO GUYS THAT WORKED FOR HIM AND AFTER BUILDING THE FIRST ONE HE WAS ABLE TO BUILD THE NEXT HOME BY HIMSELF.

A LIFETIME – GOD WILLING – IS A LONG TIME. LEARNING HOW TO DO SOMETHING DOES NOT TAKE THAT LONG, BELIEVE IT OR NOT. LOOK AROUND, THERE ARE A LOT OF DOCTORS AND LAWYERS THAT ARE ONLY IN THEIR 30'S. PRESIDENT KENNEDY WAS YOUNG WHEN HE BECAME PRESIDENT OF THE UNITED STATES. TO BE A BRAIN SURGEON TAKES A LOT OF TRAINING YET THERE ARE SOME OUT THERE WHO ARE VERY YOUNG. UNDERSTANDING ALL THERE IS TO KNOW ABOUT PLUMBING, OR ELECTRIC, OR CARPENTRY DOESN'T TAKE NEAR AS MUCH TRAINING AS BEING A BRAIN SURGEON AND YOU DON'T NEED TO KNOW EVERYTHING ABOUT PLUMBING TO PLUMB YOUR OWN HOUSE BUT YOU SHOULD GET A PLUMBER TO MAKE CERTAIN THAT IT IS CORRECT BEFORE IT IS COVERED UP AND YOU SHOULD HAVE IT INSPECTED. EVEN IF YOU ARE CURRENTLY EMPLOYED AS AN OFFICE WORKER YOU CAN GET A JOB AS A HELPER TO LEARN HOW TO DO SOMETHING THAT WILL SAVE YOU THOUSANDS AND THOUSANDS OF DOLLARS DURING YOUR LIFETIME AND YOU CAN LEARN ALL THAT YOU REALLY NEED TO KNOW IN A YEAR. WHAT IS A YEAR OUT OF A LIFETIME? I MET ONE GUY THAT OFFERED TO WORK AS A HELPER FOR A FRIEND OF MINE WHO IS IN THE AIR CONDITIONING BUSINESS FOR FREE JUST TO LEARN AIR CONDITIONING. MY FRIEND ALWAYS PAID HIM SOMETHING FOR THE WORK HE DID EVEN THOUGH HE SAID HE WOULD WORK FOR FREE. WITHIN A YEAR THE GUY WAS GETTING FULL PAY DOING THE JOB AND IN ANOTHER YEAR LEFT WORKING FOR MY FRIEND AND STARTED HIS OWN A/C BUSINESS.

YOU BOUGHT THIS BOOK BECAUSE YOU DON'T MIND A LITTLE EFFORT SO THINK ABOUT THE POSSIBILITIES AND THE OPPORTUNITIES YOU NOW KNOW ABOUT, TO LEARN A TRADE WITHOUT GOING TO COLLEGE WHICH WOULD COST YOU A LOT OF MONEY. JUST REMEMBER YOU ARE TRYING TO LEARN SOMETHING THAT WILL BE VERY VALUABLE TO YOUR FAMILY FOR THE REST OF YOUR LIFE. SINCE YOU ALREADY HAVE A JOB THAT PAYS YOUR BILLS THIS NEW JOB IS NOT A JOB – IT IS SCHOOLING – AND YOU'RE GETTING SOME MONEY TO GO TO SCHOOL.

YOU CAN BECOME WEALTHY, TOO

THE FIRST THING A CHILD MUST DO BEFORE HE CAN WALK IS TAKE THE FIRST STEP. SOON HE CAN WALK AND THEN HE CAN RUN, JUMP AND SOMEDAY MAY BECOME A GOLD MEDALIST LONG DISTANCE RUNNER.

TO BECOME WEALTHY YOU HAVE TO TAKE THE FIRST STEP AND YOU DID THAT WHEN YOU BOUGHT THIS BOOK! AFTER YOU READ IT YOU SHOULD BE ABLE TO DECIDE WHAT THE NEXT STEP IS. ONCE YOU HAVE DECIDED WHAT IT IS THEN YOU MUST PUT IT INTO ACTION BY DOING SOMETHING. IF THIS BOOK ISN'T ENOUGH THEN BUY ANOTHER ONE OR GO OUT AND GET SOME SCHOOLING BY HELPING SOMEONE BUILD A HOUSE.

YOU CAN DO IT – YOU CAN BECOME WEALTHY, TOO.

NOW YOU KNOW HOW

NOW YOU KNOW THE WAY TO BECOME WEALTHY – YOU KNOW THE WORKING MAN AND WOMANS WAY TO WEALTH! WEALTHY PEOPLE MAKE MONEY THE SAME WAY THAT YOU HAVE JUST READ ABOUT BUT THEY JUST HIRE PEOPLE TO DO EVERYTHING WE HAVE DISCUSSED IN THIS BOOK. THEY MAKE LESS MONEY OFF OF EACH HOUSE BECAUSE THEY HAVE TO PAY FOR THE WORK THAT YOU WILL BE DOING FOR YOURSELF BUT THEY STILL MAKE MONEY OR THEY WOULDN'T DO IT. THE DIFFERENCE BETWEEN YOU AND THEM IS A MATTER OF MONEY. THEY HAVE ENOUGH TO SIT IN A HOT TUB WHILE SOMEONE ELSE DOES ALL THE WORK AND YOU DON'T. YOU WORK ON A TIGHT BUDGET; EVERYTHING YOU MAKE GOES FOR BILLS, FOOD AND GASOLINE. YOU'RE BROKE RIGHT AFTER PAY DAY. THE WEALTHY PEOPLE HAVE EXTRA MONEY TO MAKE MORE MONEY WITH.

NOW YOU KNOW HOW TO HAVE EXTRA MONEY SO THAT YOU CAN USE IT TO MAKE MORE MONEY. YOU CAN LOWER YOUR EXPECTATIONS FOR FIVE OR TEN YEARS. YOU CAN KEEP THE OLD CAR, CUT OUT ON THE EXTRA TOYS, MOVE INTO A LESSER EXPENSIVE APARTMENT OR HOUSE, EAT AT HOME MORE OFTEN, DON'T BUY THAT DRESS OR NEW SUIT OR THAT SIX PACK OR WHATEVER. IT'S ONLY FOR A LITTLE WHILE AND ALL OF A SUDDEN YOU WON'T BE BROKE ANY LONGER. STOP THROWING AWAY MONEY ON RENT AS FAST AS YOU CAN! THAT WASTE ADDS UP TO A LOT OF MONEY OVER THE YEARS.

FRIENDS AND RELATIVES WILL UNDERSTAND AND THEY WILL APPRECIATE THE FACT THAT YOU ARE WILLING TO SACRAFICE A FEW COMFORTS AND TOYS TO GET SOMETHING OUT OF LIFE – TO BECOME WEALTHY. THEY MIGHT EVEN HELP YOU IF YOU JUST ASK.

REMEMBER THAT OLD 1903 LOG HOUSE THAT I BOUGHT YEARS AGO? WELL, ONE TIME I HAD A PARTY THERE BEFORE WE HAD INSTALLED THE SEWER AND WATER – WE HAD ELECTRIC THOUGH – AND SOME OF MY FRIENDS CAME. THEY DIDN'T LAUGH AT US. THEY USED THE HONEY BUCKET AND DUMPED IT IN THE PIT WE HAD DUG FOR THE WASTE. THEY RESPECTED US FOR TRYING TO GET SOMEWHERE AND FOR BEING WILLING TO SACRAFICE TO DO IT.

DO YOU KNOW HOW MUCH MONEY IT TAKES TO BE THE WEALTHIEST PERSON ON EARTH? ONE DOLLAR! IF YOU HAD ONE DOLLAR MORE THAN ANYONE ELSE ON EARTH YOU WOULD BE THE WEALTHIEST PERSON ON EARTH. ONE DOLLAR IS THE SECRET TO BECOMING WEALTHY! TO GO FROM RAGS AND FLOPPY SOLED SHOES TO WEALTHY IS DONE ONE DOLLAR AT A TIME – NOT BY MILLIONS OF DOLLARS AT A TIME, AT LEAST

NOT FOR THE WORKING MAN OR WORKING WOMAN. IF YOU WILL JUST CUT EXPENSES, STOP RENTING, STOP WASTING MONEY FOR A LITTLE WHILE YOU WILL BECOME WEALTHY BY USING WHAT YOU HAVE JUST READ.

THANK YOU AND LET ME KNOW HOW YOU ARE DOING WITH THE INFORMATION YOU JUST LEARNED.

USE THE FOLLOWING BLANK PAGES FOR SKETCHES WHEN YOU DO NOT HAVE BLANK PAPER WITH YOU WHILE MEASURING OR DOING LAYOUTS.

VISIT MY WEB SITE AT: landdirtcheap.com and click on working way to wealth